FINE ARTISTS

PRACTICAL CAREER GUIDES

Series Editor: Kezia Endsley

FINE ARTISTS

A Practical Career Guide

MARCIA SANTORE

ROWMAN & LITTLEFIELD
Lanham • Boulder • New York • London

Published by Rowman & Littlefield
An imprint of The Rowman & Littlefield Publishing Group, Inc.
4501 Forbes Boulevard, Suite 200, Lanham, Maryland 20706
www.rowman.com

6 Tinworth Street, London SE11 5AL, United Kingdom

British Library Cataloguing in Publication Information Available

Library of Congress Cataloging-in-Publication Data

Names: Santore, Marcia, 1960- author.
Title: Fine artists : a practical career guide / Marcia Santore.
Description: Lanham : Rowman & Littlefield, [2020] | Series: Practical career guides | Includes bibliographical references. | Summary: "Fine Artists: A Practical Career Guide includes interviews with professionals in the field, covers the following areas of this field that have proven to be stable, lucrative, and growing professions. · Art Media, · Conceptual Art, · Fiber Art, · Illustration, · Installation, · Mixed Media, · Murals, · New Media, · Painting, · Performance Art, · Photography, · Printmaking, · Sculpture"—Provided by publisher.
Identifiers: LCCN 2019038366 (print) | LCCN 2019038367 (ebook) | ISBN 9781538134320 (paperback) | ISBN 9781538134337 (epub)
Subjects: LCSH: Art—Vocational guidance.
Classification: LCC N8350 .S265 2020 (print) | LCC N8350 (ebook) | DDC 702.3—dc23
LC record available at https://lccn.loc.gov/2019038366
LC ebook record available at https://lccn.loc.gov/2019038367

Contents

Introduction:
So You Want a Career in Fine Art

*W*elcome to a career in fine art! Artists are a necessary part of the health and well-being of our society. Artists provide joy, inspiration, awe, and wonder. Artists also draw attention to problems in our social, economic, and political systems. Artists create and show connections between people, and between people and the natural world. Artists create community and participate in making the world a better place. Artists speak truth—of the past, of the present, and of the future. Artists show us things we would never otherwise see.

Being a fine artist is more than just a career.

"An artist's role is almost that of an Alchemist—capable of transforming a few humble materials into objects which are imbued with spiritual and aesthetic value and then possibly also material value."[1]—Aleta Michaletos

What Is an Artist?

The simplest answer is that an artist is someone who makes art. So does that mean everyone is an artist? Well, yes and no.

Many people have the creative ideas or the eye-hand coordination or the talent that we associate with artists. As the only animals that make art, humans use art to express ideas or emotions, to draw attention to visual cues in the environment that are beautiful or important, to communicate with each other, to teach, and to learn. But not everyone becomes a professional artist—or wants to. Art is something people can go on doing their entire lives, but some people are inclined to focus on other things and just do art as a life-enhancing activity.

So what drives someone to become a professional fine artist? The answer is in the question: "drive." Professional fine artists make art for all the same reasons other people do, but often there is one more element. Many artists will tell you that they don't make art because they want to, they make art because they have to. There is something inside that won't rest until they make art. Or they catch sight of something in real life that triggers that artistic impulse and is almost oppressive until it can be expressed.

Jasper Johns told of an experience like that when he glimpsed a cross-hatch pattern in the dirt on a passing car on the highway:

"I only saw it for a second, but knew immediately that I was going to use it. It had all the qualities that interest me—literalness, repetitiveness, an obsessive quality, order with dumbness, and the possibility of a complete lack of meaning."[2]—Jasper Johns

That pattern inhabited his paintings and prints for almost ten years.

THE MYTH OF THE ECCENTRIC ARTIST

There is a common myth in our society that artists are eccentrics who can't be expected to meet their responsibilities, earn a living, support a family, meet their deadlines, or otherwise act like adults. There are plenty of people who like to take advantage of that idea—who want to avoid being responsible adults by wearing eccentric clothes; drinking too much or abusing other substances; ignoring deadlines, meetings, texts, and phone calls; and thinking that by calling themselves "artists," they should be able to get away with it. While they're busy posing and watching themselves posing, they are not making any art. Whatever they are (posers, poseurs, or phonies), they aren't artists.

Artists make art and work hard at it. Artists may keep odd hours or have paint on their clothes, but they meet their obligations and responsibilities because that is the only way to advocate for their work or to have any real success in their art practice.

If you are going to be an artist, forget about trying to look like one. Forget about trying to sound like one. Forget about trying to act like one. Being an artist is not about "living an arty lifestyle." It's about making art. If you're looking at yourself instead of looking at the work, your work will suffer. Focus on making art, and your personality will take care of itself.

Can You Really Make a Living Doing That?

Yes, many people do make a living as fine artists. A tiny handful of people even become wealthy. But most fine artists pursue their art for the love of the art itself. Some artists are able to sell enough art through galleries or directly to the public to support themselves. Some artists travel the country to sell their work at outdoor art fairs. Some create specific pieces for individual collectors on commission. Some create public art for indoor or outdoor spaces. Others apply for grants to support their work. Many artists keep their fine art separate from their paid work and instead have a day job such as teaching at the elementary, secondary, or university level; working in arts administration; driving a truck; delivering mail; writing career guides; or doing something else.

There are also careers that require artistic vision and skills, such as graphic design, computer game development, and animation.

"You are fortunate enough to have a talent that can become an occupation. People want and need art. . . . Conquer the myth of the struggling artist. Get on with becoming a surviving artist in the new millennium."[3]—Constance Smith

The market for fine art depends a lot on the economy, the kind of work you make, where you live, and—more than most careers—whom you know. Personal relationships and word-of-mouth are very important for fine artists who exhibit their own work and hope to sell through galleries or directly to collectors.

No matter how you earn a living, remember that artists are entrepreneurs and small-business people. The business side of your art practice is important and no different from running any other small business. Artists who keep good records, stay organized, stay on top their finances, and are able to respond quickly and efficiently to opportunities as they arise will make more progress in their art careers while *also* having more time to make art. We'll talk more about that in chapter 4.

So let's take a look at many different fine arts media and commercial art careers and meet artists who create with different media, have different educational backgrounds, and have different artistic careers. We'll also talk about what kind of education you'll need for a career in fine art as well as how to present yourself as an artist and represent your work in college applications and in the professional art world.

Why Choose a Career in Fine Art?

Being an Artist

> "To make art is to sing with the human voice. To do this you must first learn that the only voice you need is the voice you already have."[1]—David Bayles and Ted Orland

*M*any artists will tell you that you don't choose a career as a fine artist—it chooses you.

There are many different ways to be an artist in the world. Some artists say they just make art for themselves and don't want to show it to anyone—often

Sharing your artwork with others is one of the joys of being a fine artist.

because they fear being rejected or misunderstood. But most artists want their art to communicate ideas and feelings to others. In order for that to happen, you have to get your work out in front of people, and especially art lovers and art collectors.

In this chapter, we're going to look at the personal qualities that fine artists need, some of the many kinds of art media you might want to use as a fine artist, and what kinds of jobs artists do. Throughout the book, you'll find interviews with professional visual artists. In this chapter, we'll meet the first two and see what they have to say about art and art careers.

> "Whether you succeed or not is irrelevant, there is no such thing. Making your unknown known is the important thing—and keeping the unknown always beyond you."[2]—Georgia O'Keeffe

What Qualities Do You Need to Be an Artist?

Just like other careers, if you bring certain personal qualities to the job of fine artist, you will greatly increase your chance of both artistic success and art career success.

> "Take an object / Do something to it / Do something else to it. [Repeat]."[3]—Jasper Johns

CREATIVITY

Creativity is the ability to make something new happen in the universe. Creativity is problem-solving even if in your artwork you can't (yet) define what the problem is. It means looking at things differently, considering many options, trying and discarding ideas, and then making something new out of all of it.

Talent and creativity are related but a little different. Talent is what comes naturally to you, while creativity can cross over into anything that you do.

"Talent reflects how you're hard-wired. That's what sets the concept apart from that of knowledge or skills. Talent dictates your moment-by-moment reactions to your environment—there's an instinctiveness, an immediacy implied. Talent results in consistently recurring patterns of thought or behavior. To deviate from those patterns requires conscious effort, and such deviations are difficult to sustain."[4]—Kathie Sorensen and Steve Crabtree

DRIVE

Drive is that inner feeling that pushes you to do the thing you care about most. If your drive is to make art, you'll make art. All the rejection and all the procrastination in the world won't stop you—they might slow you down, temporarily, but you will always come back to making art. Drive can be strong or quiet, fast or slow, subtle or overpowering.

"Where does this nebulous, hard-to-explain, harder-to-define quality come from, and what is it that, well, drives it? I haven't a clue. Is it essential to what you do? You bet. How will you know if you have it? Because of the way it rides you, rarely letting you rest, never letting you forget your calling. Drive is merciless, ceaseless, and in the worst cases heedless. I ought to know. I've been guilty of all that."[5]—Paul Dorrell

Why is drive important? Drive makes you make art—and that's what artists do. Drive gives you the confidence to believe in your work enough to make more. Drive makes you want to do better, to "fail up," to learn from your mistakes, to improve your skills, to delve more deeply into your ideas. Drive keeps you going even when you're tired, discouraged, and wishing you'd gone to law school. Drive drives you.

If you have the drive to make art, you won't be able to get away from it. You're an artist. You'll make art. So use that drive to your advantage—make, learn, grow, get better. Use that drive to get your work out in front of other people—for critique or for exhibition, depending on your stage of artistic development.

SKILLS

"If people knew how hard I worked to get my mastery, it wouldn't seem so wonderful at all."[6]—Michelangelo

To make your best art, you need to have control of your materials and know how to get them to do what you want. There are too many art skills to list all of them here, but you can get better at any of them by doing these things.

1. **Learn:** One of the best ways to learn an art skill is to have someone who knows what they're doing show you and correct your mistakes. So take a class or work with a master artist to learn a new art skill.
2. **Practice:** Repetition is the key to mastering any skill. So practice your art technique over and over again until you can do it almost without thinking.
3. **Challenge yourself:** After you have some mastery of a skill, ask yourself what else there is to know. How you can take this skill to the next level?
4. **Learn more:** Take an advanced class or work with a master artist to enhance the skill you've learned.
5. **Practice more:** Keep practicing! The more you use your new and enhanced skills, the better they'll get.
6. **Challenge yourself more:** What else could you do with this skill? Use your creativity to take your work even higher by coming up with something to do with this art skill all on your own. And practice.

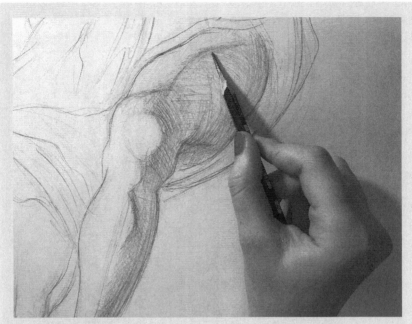

Observational drawing is an important skill for all artists to cultivate.

The one skill every artist needs is drawing from life. Whatever kind of art you do—strict realism or the most out-there conceptualism—being able to draw from your own observation is a skill you need.

Observational drawing is drawing real three-dimensional things—people, objects, landscapes, buildings, whatever—not from a photograph or your imagination. It's a skill that anyone can learn (although some people seem to have been born with the ability) and that anyone can improve on.

What do you learn from all that observational drawing from life?

- How to translate from your eye to your hand.
- Control of your materials.
- The difference between the important and the unimportant—what to include and what to exclude.
- Proportion, composition, anatomy, and perspective.
- Creative decision-making—what do you put in a thirty-second drawing versus a thirty-minute drawing or a three-hour drawing?

PERSISTENCE

Persistence means you keep going. As an artist, you'll need persistence at every level, from learning art skills to finishing artwork to building a consistent body of work to getting your work in front of people. Persistence means pushing forward when outside influences are pushing back.

The good news is that persistence is a skill that you can teach yourself. So how do you become persistent?

1. Know your goals: It's easier to keep moving if you can see where you're going.
2. Keep your goals reachable: How do you eat an elephant? One bite at a time. Don't frighten yourself with large, distant goals like "Have a solo exhibition at the Museum of Modern Art in New York." Focus on the next thing you need to do—start a piece, finish a piece, or turn an assignment in on time, for example.
3. Know your priorities: You already know what your priorities are. Get your school work done. Get your work work done. Hang with your friends. Call your mom. Make art. Not necessarily in that order.
4. Make art a priority: Make making art a priority in your life. Carve out time in your schedule for the studio.
5. Use positive self-talk: Don't let your inner voice give you a hard time. We all have a nasty little inner voice that makes us doubt ourselves (see the sidebar "Doubt"). Sometimes your inner voice tells you to watch TV or play video games instead of making art. Counter that voice by purposefully talking to yourself in a supportive and positive way. No, not out loud. Tell yourself, "I'm just going to do this now."
6. Get in the habit of getting in the habit: Pick a thing and do it. Then pick another thing, and do that. Repeat.
7. Notice when you finish: Pay attention to those special times when you complete a project. Feel proud of yourself. See how nice that is? Noticing how good it feels to finish something helps you be persistent in the future.

"In spite of everything I shall rise again: I will take up my pencil, which I have forsaken in my great discouragement, and I will go on with my drawing."[7]—Vincent Van Gogh

PATIENCE

Art takes patience at every stage. Patience doesn't mean sitting around waiting for opportunities to come to you. Patience means accepting that things take time and that fretting and stressing about it doesn't make things happen any sooner. Patience means accepting that if one opportunity doesn't work out, there is always another one.

When you are a student artist, it will take time for you to develop your work to the point where it is good enough to exhibit. You need to have patience with yourself while you are learning and have patience with your work while you are "growing up" as an artist.

Every artist, at every level, makes pieces that don't turn out. Have patience with yourself and your work. Let the poor ones go—don't agonize over them. Let the good ones shine. If you're not sure, put the piece away for a while. Have patience and look at it again in a month or so to see what you think.

Developing a career in fine art takes a lot of patience. You'll need to be patient while you wait to hear if you've been accepted by the school of your choice or for a particular exhibition. You'll need to be patient during critiques. You'll need to be patient while seeking opportunities throughout your career.

HAVE FAITH IN YOURSELF AND YOUR ARTWORK

Perhaps the most important quality artists need to have is faith in themselves as artists and faith in their work. Some people seem to be born confident or talented or both. Others need to develop it over the course of a lifetime.

Faith in yourself and your artwork doesn't mean arrogance or the assumption that you have nothing new or different to learn. It means an internal confidence in your ability to learn, to imagine, and to create that will carry you through difficult times. It means learning to recognize what is good in your work yourself without relying only on the opinions of others. It also means

Confidence in yourself and your artwork helps keep you going as a fine artist.

being confident enough in your abilities to recognize when a piece is not working so that you can either fix it or set it aside and move on to something else.

DOUBT

"What if I'm not good enough?"

"What if I'm not talented enough?"

"Why doesn't my work look like X's?"

"Why don't I have good ideas like X does?"

"What if I'm just fooling myself?"

"What if I should have gone to law school?"

All artists ask themselves these questions or similar questions throughout their careers. So when you hear the nasty little voice of doubt whispering in your ear, take heart! You're not alone. Doubt talks to everyone like that.

Sometimes doubt is useful. Doubt can be challenging you to improve. The only way to answer doubts like "What if I'm not good enough?" or

"What if I'm not talented enough?" or "What if I'm just fooling myself?" is another question: "How can I make *this piece* better?"

Why doesn't your work look like X's or have X's ideas? Because it's not X's work. It's your work! Make it the best *your work* that you can. Remember, while you're worrying about X, he or she is worrying about Y, and Q is worrying about you.

If you want to go to law school, that path is not closed to you. Neither is the path of being a good and worthwhile artist.

Tell the nasty little voice of doubt to take off, and then get back to making art. As Vincent van Gogh said, "If you hear a voice within you saying, 'You are not a painter,' then by all means paint, boy, and that voice will be silenced."[8]

Art Media

There are more types of art media than could possibly fit in this book. Let's take a look at some of the ways of making art that are out there in the world. These are in alphabetical order—no particular way of making art is any more or less important than any other.

CONCEPTUAL ART

In conceptual art, the ideas take precedence over how an artwork looks, lasts, or is made. Installation and performance art (listed below) often fall into the category of conceptual art. Conceptual artists usually resist the idea of art as a commodity—something to be bought and sold. Conceptual art can be used to tell stories, to bring attention to marginalized communities, and to protest social problems like sexism and racism.

Conceptual art can leave you with the idea that traditional art skills aren't necessary, but many conceptual artists rely on those skills, as well as performance skills, to create conceptual artwork. Some conceptual pieces have a physical form that exists in space and is made to continue over time (and that, ironically, can be bought and sold). Other conceptual art is intended to be ephemeral—although traces can be found in photos and video.

Some of the most important names in conceptual art include

- John Baldessari
- Vanessa Beecroft
- Marcel Duchamp
- Tracey Emin
- Andrea Fraser
- Jenny Holzer
- Douglas Huebler
- Joseph Kosuth

- Annette Lemieux
- Sol LeWitt
- N. E. Thing Co. Ltd.
- Edward Ruscha
- Rhea Sue Sanders
- Gillian Wearing
- Lawrence Weiner
- xurban collective

There are even more listed under "Installation" and "Performance Art" below.

DRAWING

Drawing is making marks to create a form, shape, or image by using something that leaves a mark on a surface. That could be charcoal, pencil, color pencil, pen and ink, markers, pastels, chalk, or pixels, for example. Drawing can be realistic, abstract, linear, volumetric, academic, gestural, sketchy, detailed—whatever you want it to be.

Some artists use drawing as the basis for painting, print-making, or other media. Some artists use drawing to plan large works such as sculptures or installations. Drawing can be used to tell stories—as in children's books, comic books, cartoons, anime, and manga. Or drawing can just be an art form in its own right.

Some artists who have done amazing things with drawing include

- Jean-Michel Basquiat
- Aubrey Beardsley
- Virginia Lee Burton
- Mary Cassatt
- Leonardo da Vinci
- Albrecht Dürer
- M. C. Escher
- Eva Hesse
- Käthe Kollwitz
- Michelangelo

- Hayao Miyazaki
- Tamarin Norwood
- Pablo Picasso
- Beatrix Potter
- Arthur Rackham
- Rembrandt van Rijn
- Patricia Schappler
- Egon Schiele
- E. H. Shephard
- Cy Twombly

FIBER ART

Fiber art is fine art constructed from natural or synthetic fiber, including fabric or yarn. The focus is more on the significance of the materials and the artist's process rather than utility. Quilting, embroidery, weaving, tapestry, knitting, crocheting, sewing, and wearable art are just some of the fiber art possibilities. Some fiber artists add beading or dye or print their own fibers or fabric.

This is an art form that often overlaps with traditional crafts such as sewing, basketry, and quilting. Many fiber artists today are actively seeking to elevate the medium as a feminist statement regarding the long history of fiber art and craft as "women's work."

Well-known fiber artists include both men and women. If you are interested in learning more about fiber art, here are a dozen artists who are all doing very different things with fiber.

- Faig Ahmed
- El Anatsui
- Nick Cave
- Steven Frost
- Mascha Mioni
- Laura Morrison
- Faith Ringold
- Miriam Schapiro
- Izziyana Suhaimi
- Kazuhito Takadoi
- Joana Vasconcelos
- Cookie Washington

ILLUSTRATION

Illustration means creating images that enhance or explain a text. The text can be anything from a children's book to a magazine article to an anatomy book for medical students to an illuminated manuscript. Illustrations can be made using drawing and painting, of course. But thanks to photography and digital programs like Adobe Illustrator and Photoshop, illustrations can now be created using any art medium, including collage, montage, embroidery, multimedia, digital originals, and even 3-D techniques.

There are a number of different fields that need illustrators. Some are more creative, and some help convey technical or scientific ideas. Here is a short list of the kinds of jobs illustrators do.

- Archeological illustration
- Architectural illustration /rendering
- Book illustration
- Botanical illustration
- Character design
- Concept art
- Cover art for books or CDs
- Fashion illustration
- Graphic novels
- Information graphics
- Medical illustration
- Narrative illustration
- Scientific illustration
- Technical illustration
- Video game art

INSTALLATION

Tate defines installation art this way:

> The term "installation art" is used to describe large-scale, mixed-media constructions, often designed for a specific place or for a temporary period of time . . . Installation artworks (also sometimes described as "environments") often occupy an entire room or gallery space that the spectator has to walk through in order to engage fully with the work of art. Some installations, however, are designed simply to be walked around and contemplated, or are so fragile that they can only be viewed from a doorway, or one end of a room. What makes installation art different from sculpture or other traditional art forms is that it is a complete unified experience, rather than a display of separate, individual artworks. The focus on how the viewer experiences the work and the desire to provide an intense experience for them is a dominant theme in installation art.[9]

Environmental art and earthworks are often included in the installation category. Because installation art is on a large scale and is usually temporary, these pieces are rarely sold to collectors, although some become part of a museum's permanent collection. Grant funding is often necessary to support the creation of a large installation piece so that the artist's ideas can be realized without having to respond to market forces.

Some well-known installations artists include

- Judy Chicago
- Christo and Jeanne-Claude
- Yayoi Kusama
- Sharon Louden
- Gordon Matta-Clark
- Bruce Naumann
- Doris Salcedo
- Robert Smithson
- Kara Walker
- Ai Weiwei

MIXED MEDIA

Whenever an artist uses more than one kind of art medium in a single piece, it is called "mixed media." Some artists might combine graphite, paint, and wood into a single painting. It's a painting, but it's also mixed media. A quilter might include printing and beads or other small objects in his or her quilt. It's a quilt, but it's also mixed media. Found objects are often important in mixed-media work. They can inspire an artist to create a work by combining the found item with others and with more traditional art media.

Some art forms only exist as mixed media. Collage is a two-dimensional or low-relief medium in which paper, cloth, photographs, and other things are attached to a flat surface. Collage can be enhanced with paint or drawing. Assemblage is a 3-D medium where objects are attached to a board or placed inside a box. Altered books are made by taking an existing book and adding and subtracting material to create an artwork.

Some well-known mixed-media artists include

- Ifeoma Anyaeji
- George Braque
- Rhea Carmi
- Joseph Cornell
- Njideka Akunyili Crosby
- Marcel Duchamp
- Sudobh Gupta
- Jasper Johns
- Edward Kienholz
- Louise Nevelson
- Meret Oppenheim
- Pablo Picasso
- Robert Rauschenberg
- Thomas Wesselmann

MURALS

The term "mural" refers to any painting that is created directly on a wall. These can include a wall-sized painting in a home, a business, or a public space. Murals can be painted in any style. For instance, graffiti is a type of mural. Murals are frequently created for public spaces and thus can invoke a sense of civic, regional, national, or ethnic pride.

Because many murals are outside, it's important to understand the effect of weather and the environment on this kind of work. Some murals are painted on a separate surface such as plywood or metal and then affixed to the building. Some are painted directly on the wall.

Murals bring art and pride to communities.

Funding for murals comes from grants, individual donors, communities, and percent-for-art programs. Mural artists often work with schools or after-school art programs to create a work, which is a great learning experience for the kids and helps build a sense of ownership in the mural for the community.

Some notable muralists include

- Dorothy Annan
- Thomas Hart Benton
- Blek le Rat
- Keith Haring
- Iz the Wiz
- Susan Krieg
- Will Hicok Low
- Sofia Maldonado
- José Clemente Orozco
- Diego Rivera
- P. K. Sadanandan
- Lucia Wiley

NEW MEDIA ART

New media art is created using digital or new technology. It can include digital art, computer graphics and animation, virtual art, Internet art, art for video games or robotics, 3-D printing, and more. New media art often involves some kind of interaction between the artist, the medium, and the audience. New media art overlaps with many other art forms, including digital art, conceptual art, performance art, and systems art, for example.

To learn more about art being made using new media, check out some of these artists:

- Deborah Aschheim
- Jeremy Blake
- Nia Burks
- Shu Lea Cheang
- Ursula Endlicher
- Floating Point Unit
- G. H. Hovagimyan
- Knifeandfork
- Nam June Paik
- VNS Matrix

PAINTING

Painting is sometimes the first type of work people think of when they hear the word "art." Painting is simply the act of placing pigment suspended in a medium (such as oil, acrylic, wax, egg, etc.) on a surface with some sort of implement (such as a brush, your fingers, a stick, a palette knife, or something else). Artists who are painters often incorporate drawing in their paintings and sometimes include other materials. We usually think of painting as applying oil or acrylic paint to a canvas or watercolors to paper with a brush. Painters work in a wide variety of styles, from photographic realism to complete abstraction and everything in between.

Painters may work on canvas, wood, paper, or other substrates. Common painting media include

- acrylic
- enamel
- encaustic
- gouache
- ink
- oil
- spray paint
- tempera
- watercolor

PATRICIA SCHAPPLER—PAINTER

Patricia Schappler and *Coming and Going*, a mixed-media piece using charcoal, graphite, acrylic, photo transfer, and collage.

Patricia Schappler, BFA, MFA, is an artist working in drawing, painting, and mixed media. She has appeared in numerous solo and group exhibitions, and she has won many awards for her work. She has taught painting and drawing at the New Hampshire Institute of Art; Rivier University; Nashua Center for the Arts; and Montserrat College. She lives in Bedford, New Hampshire. Her work can be seen at www.patriciaschappler.com, on her Instagram feed @patriciaschappler, and at www.saatchiart.com.

What kind of art do you make?

I make representational figure drawings and paintings. The human form with the narrative of home and how we shift through time and event are part of the discoveries that become focal through gesture, pattern, scale, and color.

How long have you been an artist?

I've been making art since I was a child. I was a quiet kid, and drawing was a way to be still, to observe and understand my siblings, parents, and extended family. I became seriously focused in college, so that places me making art for a bit over thirty years in and around raising my family.

Did you always intend to be an artist or did it happen later?

I loved the humanities broadly including literature, psychology, sociology, and the visual arts. I began college at the University of New Hampshire without a declared major and focused on human development and sociology, which continue to have their impact on my thought process in creating work. During the second semester of my second undergraduate year, I began taking art courses and declared my major as a BFA in drawing.

How did you learn your art?

I studied under Sigmund Abeles, Carol Aronson Shore, and Scott Schnepf in undergraduate studies at the University of New Hampshire and worked with Lennart Anderson and Sam Gelber in my graduate program at Brooklyn College. I believe I gravitated toward those teachers I saw myself in philosophically and that the growth of my work is a dedicated mix of enthusiastic mentoring, self-discipline, and enough heart to lead to process and voice.

How did (or didn't) your education prepare you for the different aspects of the job of artist?

At the time, instruction was less focused on professional entry into the world. There was a large learning curve for understanding postgrad needs including how to present one's works, how to interview, how to choose spaces that fit the work, how to market. This created challenges. However, my education encouraged a solid, traditional grasp of observational techniques, a working knowledge of art history in context with my own work, and a growing awareness of the expressive power of the arts to affect awareness, empathy, and change. Today, instructors continue traditional and contemporary approaches, expand art historical references much more broadly, open cross-media dialogues, and offer varied professional workshops on campuses, creating a stronger, healthier understanding of both the creative and business side of art making.

What other jobs do you/did you do in addition to being an artist?

I had many jobs! In high school, college, and through graduate work, I waitressed and was a hostess, worked in an art store, performed administrative and secretarial work, tutored, did visual merchandising, illustrated children's educational pamphlets, taught English as a second language, created commissioned work, and taught adults and children at the local art centers. A couple of years postgrad, I began teaching at the college level including Montserrat College, Rivier University, and the New Hampshire Institute of Art.

What's the best part of being an artist?

There are many wonderful parts, including the art community, so it's difficult to pick one. Perhaps the most magical is that process informs discoveries about the people I work from, the world I live in, and my understanding of self. Empathy, patience, generosity, and love thrive in the process of creating.

What's the worst part of being an artist?

You have to finance your time in the studio through something, frequently through . . . grants, sales, instruction, etc., but generally speaking, work has to be seen and it has to be sold. The business side of remaining organized and true to your own voice is challenging. Creative people want to spend their time in the studio making rather than managing where the art goes once completed. Framing, photographing, dating, titling, answering emails, finding appropriate venues to show work, insuring, packaging, and sending images out are time consuming and can feel incredibly interruptive.

What's the most surprising thing about being an artist?

The act of making is an act of optimism, a belief in creativity, a letting go of control to discover, and a stretching of sensitivity. It is an innate and beautifully human act.

What advice would you give a young person who wants to be an artist?

Get up and work, and play, and be in the moment—you'll find what you need through all of it. Playing, doing, seeing is the fun side of discovery—working in the studio is less predictably satisfying. Don't reach for formula. Reach for your best voice, reach for your peers and dialogue, reach for the consistency of trying. Be part of the art community, find homes for your work, critique with your peers, boost yourself through engagement. Work through the ugly, difficult, can't-find-your-way days the same way you work through the easy, fluid days—with encouragement and purpose.

PERFORMANCE ART

Performance art is different from the performing arts. Performance art is a kind of conceptual art that consists of the actions of a person or group at a particular place and time. This can be in a gallery or in some other kind of space. It can be scripted or not, planned or improvised. It can involve people, video, sound, time, space, and a relationship between the artist and the audience.

Some performance artists to know about include

- Marina Abramović
- Vito Acconci
- Laurie Anderson
- Joseph Beuys
- Chris Burden
- Diogenes
- Karen Finley
- Gilbert & George
- Tehching Hseih
- Zhang Huan
- Yves Klein
- Linda Montano
- Yoko Ono
- Carolee Schneemann

PHOTOGRAPHY

Art photographers create works of art using film and digital photography, in color or in black-and-white. In addition to selling their art photographs, photographers can also use this skill to support themselves as photojournalists, portrait photographers, and wedding photographers.

Both film and digital photographs can be manipulated by the photographer to make them look the way he or she wants. In addition, camera lenses themselves create distortions. A photograph does not really "capture reality." The photographer makes choices about composition, light versus dark, color, and countless other details.

Some well-known photographer-artists include

- Ansel Adams
- Diane Arbus
- Henri Cartier-Bresson
- John William Draper
- Walker Evans
- Lotte Jacobi
- Barbara Kasten
- André Kertész
- Dorothea Lange
- Man Ray
- Robert Mapplethorpe
- Joseph Neumann
- Gordon Parks
- Susan Rankaitis
- Cindy Sherman
- Edward Steichen
- Carrie Mae Weems
- William Wegman
- Garry Winogrand

PRINTMAKING

The Metropolitan Museum of Art gives this succinct description of printmaking:

> Printmaking is an artistic process based on the principle of transferring images
> from a matrix onto another surface, most often paper or fabric. . . . A matrix
> is essentially a template, and can be made of wood, metal, or glass. The design
> is created on the matrix by working its flat surface with either tools or chem-
> icals. The matrix is then inked in order to transfer it onto the desired surface.
> To print from a matrix requires the application of controlled pressure.[10]

Printing is a way to create multiple copies of an artwork that are each
artworks in themselves. The artist controls the number of copies produced
for a limited edition of prints and then signs and numbers each copy. Digital
art prints are artworks that are created using digital media. These are usually
printed on archival paper using an archival inkjet printer. Many people confuse
digital art prints with giclée prints or other reproduction or poster techniques.

A short list of printing techniques includes

- aquatint
- digital
- dry point
- engraving
- etching
- foam plate
- foil imaging

- linoleum block
- lithography
- mezzotint
- monoprint
- monotype
- serigraphy
- woodcut

SCULPTURE

Sculpture is three-dimensional art, including everything from representational
statues to abstract forms and almost-two-dimensional reliefs. Along with petro-
glyphs (lines carved in stone) and cave paintings, sculpture is one of the oldest
art forms we know about: the Venus of Berekhat Ram, a stone figurine discov-
ered in the hills north of Israel, dates from between 230,000 and 500,000 BCE.
Today, sculptors use both traditional and new methods to create their work.
Here's a short list of available sculpture materials:

- Bone, antler, ivory, shell
- Clay
- Fabric
- Glass
- Metal (bronze, steel, copper, etc.)
- Paper
- Plaster
- Plastic (e.g., 3-D printing)
- Recycled materials
- Sand
- Stone (marble, alabaster, soapstone, limestone, granite, etc.)
- Wax
- Wire
- Wood

"So why do we make art? Why is art so important to us? It's simple. Because we enjoy it. In fact, we live for it. Few in life have this type of passion for a certain thing, particularly something that's so enjoyable. It was given to us at birth, and it drives us forward."[11]—Lee Hammond

Art Jobs and Day Jobs

For an artist, it would be great to make a living making art and selling it to collectors. That can happen—we'll talk about that at greater length in the next chapter. But not everyone can make a living that way—or at least, not at first. Almost all fine artists have to have a day job to support making art.

There are advantages and disadvantages to having a day job, of course. Advantages include things like a regular income, vacations and holidays, health insurance, a retirement plan, and a regular schedule. Disadvantages include time away from the studio, an inflexible schedule, and a lack of freedom to let your mind wander, to go see art, to hang with other artists, and to think of new artworks to make.

"A celebrated sculptor, [Richard] Serra teamed up with fellow New York City art buddies in the 1960s to found Low-Rate Movers. Employees included painter Chuck Close, monologist Spalding Grey, and the ever-industrious Philip Glass. They shared a van and mainly moved furniture. 'It was a good job because none of us would work more than two or three days a week, so we had the remaining days to do our own work,' Serra said."[12]—Clay Wirestone

ART-RELATED JOBS

Here's a quick glance at some of the jobs that artists do to support themselves, their families, and their work while bringing their creative vision to life in their artwork. In chapter 2, we'll go into more detail on how to prepare yourself for jobs like these.

Teaching

One of the most common day jobs for artists is teaching. Some artists get a degree in art education and teach in elementary, middle, or high school. Some artists get a master of fine arts (MFA) degree, which is equivalent to a doctorate in another field and is the necessary credential to teach art at the college or university level. Art teaching can be a great way to be thinking about art while working.

Commercial Art

Artists can stay connected to their creativity by working as graphic artists or illustrators, art directors, character and concept artists, animators, industrial designers, or background and model artists for the movie industry, for example.

Gallery/Museum Staff

Some artists work for art galleries, art centers, or museums. You'll be surrounded by art and artists all the time while learning the ins and outs of art exhibitions. If you're interested in this kind of work, try volunteering at a local museum or gallery while you're still in school.

Art Therapy

Art therapy is a growing field that lets you combine your artistic talents with an opportunity to help others.

Artist's Assistant

When you're first starting out or still in school, working as an artist's assistant will give you real-life, hands-on experience in what it means to work as a pro-

There are jobs for artists in the art world, in education, and in business.

fessional artist as well as a chance to meet people in your art community. Sometimes these are paid positions, and sometimes they are available as internships.

NON-ART JOBS

Of course, you don't have to have an art-related job. Some artists find that they like having a non-art job so that when they're in the studio, they're focused only on their own artwork. Meanwhile, being out in the world and doing another kind of work refreshes their minds and refills their creative coffers.

What are some other jobs that artists can do? Just about anything! Artists have worked as

- administrative assistants
- apartment managers
- authors
- bank tellers
- commodities brokers
- cooks
- doctors

- editors
- electricians
- engineers
- event coordinators
- fundraisers
- house painters
- lawyers

- nannies
- plumbers
- police officers
- politicians
- postal workers

- retail clerks
- sales managers
- technical writers
- waiters
- writers

You name it, they've done it!

WHAT IS SUCCESS FOR AN ARTIST?

Success in most careers is easy to define: get a job, move up the ladder, make more money—you set specific goals and you achieve them. On the other hand, artists have two distinct kinds of success that may or may not go together.

1. Success as an artist means producing your best work consistently throughout your career. Success as an artist does not mean every piece succeeds, but it means you have reached the point where you can tell the difference, and you only put your best work out into the world. Success as an artist comes from growing and developing in your work—going through the lifelong process of exploration and discovery that is what creative work is.

2. Having a successful art career is more like a successful career in any other field. People know your work and want to support it, either by collecting it, selling it, or providing grant funding to allow you to continue making it. You decide for yourself what level of art career success "counts" for you. If you take a booth at an outdoor community art fair and sell half your pieces, you have achieved one kind of successful art career. If you have a solo exhibition at the Museum of Modern Art in New York City, you have achieved a different kind of successful art career. Both are valid, depending on what you want from your career and for your life.

Remember: these two kinds of success are not connected to each other. You can make the best art in the world (success as an artist), but if nobody ever sees it, you cannot have a successful art career. Make your best work, advocate for your work, and don't worry about what people with more successful art careers are doing. There will always be someone with a more successful art career than yours, just as there will always be someone with a less successful art career. But you are the only one who can make your artwork.

HOW ARE JOB PROSPECTS FOR ARTISTS?

Artists of all kinds sell their work to collectors and work on commission to create pieces that a specific client is looking for. Many artists support themselves with other jobs—such as teaching art or working for an arts organization.

Most artists make art for reasons beyond jobs or commerce, so "job prospects" is a fuzzy idea for artists. If they can sell their work, great. Or they might receive grants for certain projects. Or they can have a day job to support themselves and their work. We'll go into more detail about that in chapter 2.

Art prices vary so widely (depending on how well-known the artist is and how much work they sell in a year) that it's hard to pinpoint a reliable average. Let's look at portrait painting as an example. A painter who's just starting out might charge $1,000 for a portrait, while an established portrait artist might charge $15,000 to $25,000 or more.

In the next chapter, you'll learn how to prepare yourself for a career in the fine arts.

SHARON LOUDON—INSTALLATION ARTIST

Installation artist Sharon Loudon (left). Photo by Vinson Valega. Windows at the University of Wyoming Art Museum (right) installed in Laramie, Wyoming. Photo by Chris Gallo.

Sharon M. Louden is an artist, educator, and advocate for artists living in Queens, New York, and she works at DUMBO in Brooklyn. She holds a BFA from the Art Institute of Chicago and an MFA from Yale University School of Art. Her work is held in major public and private collections including the Whitney Museum of American

Art, National Gallery of Art, Neuberger Museum of Art, Arkansas Arts Center, Yale University Art Gallery, Weatherspoon Art Museum, and Museum of Fine Arts, Houston. She is a faculty member in the MFA Fine Arts program at the School of Visual Arts in New York. Sharon Loudon is the editor of *Living and Sustaining a Creative Life: Essays by 40 Working Artists* (2013). You can learn more about her and her work at www.sharonlouden.com and www.livesustain.org.

What kind of art do you make?

I'm a multidisciplinary artist who engages in many different kinds of art work and collaborations.

Did you always intend to be an artist or did it happen later?

I was born an artist, I think. That sounds really cliché, I know, but it's true. I never thought about it.

How did you learn your art?

I think technique is very important—technique that's harmonious with ideas. How does anyone learn how to use material? You dive into it, you seek advice from others, you go to school, you listen to your community.

What drew you to making installations?

I wanted to create inclusive environments that add architecture for engagement with viewers.

How did (or didn't) your education prepare you for the different aspects of the job of artist?

I think every source of education has prepared me to be an artist: the examples by others that have given me the confidence to make art in the public realm, the examples of women I've studied with to not hold back my point, the artists of the past who've showed me that art is a form of freedom of expression.

What other jobs do you/did you do in addition to being an artist?

There's no such thing as a "day job" because even if I have a job, I'm still an artist. I have bartended, I have made Dominos pizzas, I shined shoes at airports, I have worked in libraries, I've worked as a registrar in continuing education, I've taught, and I've gotten a few grants (but not many).

What's the best part of being an artist?

The freedom to express myself and the community in which I live. Community engagement and artists sharing with other artists really works. Working with many systems is what makes an art career sustainable. It's a matter of cultural reciprocity and exchange. Even working with a gallery dealer is a collaboration, not a singular endeavor.

What's the worst part of being an artist?

The struggle to fight against and educate those who do not or cannot see our value. Art is everywhere—it's essential to our being. Respect for the value of the creative arts should be embedded in our education system so that artists receive the resources we need to make what we provide to society.

What advice would you give a young person who wants to be an artist?

You can sustain a creative life. You have to be mindful of the lack of value that is out in the world, however. You have to mine communities and resources that are around you and create community around you in order to be successful.

Forming a Career Plan in Fine Art

Preparing for a Fine Art Career

Fine artists are professionals who can fill many roles.

A career in fine art can take many forms, and there are different roads that lead to each of those types of careers. You might have a career as an exhibiting fine artist, showing and selling your work in galleries in major cities like New York or London. You might travel the country, selling artwork directly to the public from your own booth at outdoor art fairs and festivals. You might create work on commission, such as portraits, pet portraits, murals, or sculpture. You'll probably also have a day job to support yourself while you build or carry out your art career. To be successful at any of those jobs, you'll need to develop one superimportant skill: *building relationships.*

Building Relationships

More than most other careers, a fine art career runs on personal relationships. The most reliable way to join a gallery, for instance, is for another artist to recommend you. You'll have all kinds of professional and nonprofessional relationships in the art world—friends, colleagues, mentors, and partners. As an artist, you will be an important participant in your community, and you will get to collaborate with all sorts of people from all walks of life on all kinds of projects.

> "Every artist feels alone and isolated. Friends are very important in terms of all sorts of definitions of oneself. They tell you what you are and what they are aside from the intellectual aspects."[1]—Jasper Johns

Relationships are at the heart of success in the art world.

It's easy to meet other artists while you're in school, but it can be more difficult when you're on your own or in a new community. So how do you meet like-minded artists and the art world's movers and shakers? This can feel daunting—especially if you tend to be more introverted. Here are some ways to get to know people in your art community.

Go to art gallery and museum openings. If you really don't like crowds, at least stay long enough to shake hands with the gallery director, meet the artist or artists, and say hello to anyone who looks familiar. Look for opportunities to introduce yourself and talk with people. Showing up is important: people will become familiar with your face and name and will consider you part of the scene.

Visit art galleries during the day. If you can visit a gallery during the middle of a weekday, it will be quieter and you will have a better chance to look at the art.

- Be sure to greet whoever is working in the gallery.
- Be friendly but professional.
- Do not ask for anything (like an appointment to show them your work)!
- If you know someone who knows someone at the gallery, see if they'll come with you and make an introduction.

Go to open studios! Meet the artists, see whose work resonates with yours, pick up their business card, and leave your own. Or host an open studio and invite everyone you can think of—whether you know them or not!

Join artist groups. Joining an artist group is a great way to meet other artists.

- Look for groups of artists who have something in common with you already. If you do large conceptual video installations, you might not have much in common with a group that's focused on oil paintings of the Rocky Mountains. But maybe you do!
- Keep an open mind and be friendly. Sometimes certain artists view all other artists as competitors and are less than welcoming. But most artists appreciate the chance to talk to others who share their interests.
- Participate in group activities and exhibitions—and do a little more than just include your work. Help develop the invitation list, plan the reception, pick up and deliver art. There is always something that needs

doing. If you're reliable and helpful, everyone will remember who you are.

Learn something new. Take additional art classes to help you build and develop your artwork. Or learn about business practices for artists, how to find grants, how to photograph your work, and many other topics. You'll meet other artists seeking the same information.

- Creative Capital, based in New York City, holds career-development workshops for artists on topics like financial literacy, funding your work, documenting performances, and promoting your work. Some are held online, and some are held in person.
- State arts councils often host workshops for artists on professional skills or their percent-for-art programs and grants.
- Americans for the Arts' Local Arts Network has resources and training tools to help you become a local leader in the arts as well as other programs such as an arts and business partnership program, the pARTnership Movement.

Help someone. Look for opportunities to volunteer at local galleries and museums. Offer to teach an art class for underprivileged children or seniors. It feels great to help others, and it gets your name out there in connection with art. Is your neighbor at the local arts-in-the-park festival struggling with their tent? Lend a hand.

Say yes. When an opportunity comes up, say yes. If someone invites you to be part of a show, or to talk about your work, or to come to their open studio, gallery opening, or party—say yes. When an opportunity comes your way, say yes. Okay, there will be some things you need to say no to, but in general, look for the chance to say yes.

"Over many years as an arts educator, I have helped people and communities find their voices and express their concerns through individual and collaborative art projects. This used to be called public art. Now, it is often known as social practice."[2]—Ginny Sykes

Showing Your Artwork

Chapter 1 covered different kinds of fine art and artists. Now let's consider what a career in fine art consists of. We'll start with the many ways artists can get their artwork in front of viewers.

⋅ Why do artists show their work? One reason is to sell it. But artists whose work isn't intended to be sold still want to show their work. So why do we go to all the time, trouble, and expense of exposing our beloved artwork to strangers?

Making art is an act of communication. A piece isn't really finished until it reaches its audience. The only way your artwork can find its audience is if you,

Exhibiting your best artwork is a way to communicate your ideas to viewers.

the artist, help it go out into the world. So showing your work is much more than just saying "Look what I made!" It's about advocating for your work by facilitating its relationship with the viewer.

In addition, there are certain ways of presenting your work that are "the norm" for the art world, including your artist's résumé or CV, your statement, and other documentation. We're going to talk more about that in chapter 4.

WHAT WILL YOU SHOW?

That's easy. Only your best work—the best of *your best*, right here, right now. That's only fair to your work. It doesn't have to be perfect. It doesn't even have to be what you had in mind when you started the piece (in fact, it most likely won't be).

It's also important to show a consistent body of work. If you are having a solo exhibit, are one of just a few artists in an exhibition, or are presenting an exhibition proposal, it's important to stick to artwork that works well together as a group or a series. The same goes for selling work in a booth at an art fair. Let your style show.

Does that mean you should only do one kind of art? Of course not! Do as many kinds of art as you want to! Make lots of different pieces in as many series as you want to! That's one of the perks of being a fine artist—nobody but you gets to decide what you make. BUT when you *show* your work, group like with like and show them together. The sidebar "Are Your Ready to Show Your Artwork?" offers some questions to ask yourself.

ARE YOU READY TO SHOW YOUR ARTWORK?

How do you know if you're ready to show your artwork? Ask yourself these questions.

Is my work good enough? Only you can answer this question. There will always be someone out there who thinks your work isn't good enough (they may be right, but they may be wrong). The real question is "Is my work *as good as I can make it?*" If you see room for improvement—improve. If you think you can do better—do better.

Do I have a consistent body of work? Be sure to choose pieces that look like they were made by the same artist. When you show your artworks together, look for themes, materials, or formal elements that tie the work together.

Is my work physically ready to put in a show? This is a much more practical question. Make sure the answer is yes.

- 2-D, wall-hung work must be at least wired for hanging. Does it also need a frame? Is the wire strong enough to hold the weight of the piece?
- If you're showing an assemblage, be sure all the pieces are secure so that nothing falls off when someone else is handling the piece.
- Does your sculpture need a pedestal? If the venue doesn't have one, be ready to bring your own.
- Is your oil painting dry? It better be.

Am I ready mentally and emotionally? Probably not—but you don't have to be. Do it anyway. If you haven't shown your work before, you'll likely be pretty nervous. You're putting what you care about most out in front of other people. Will they like it? Get it? Judge it? Will they even notice it? Will anyone show up? Even if the answer to all these questions turns out to be no, what's the worst that can happen? It won't feel good, but you'll survive and live to show another day. Chances are some people will like it, some will get it, others may judge it, most will notice it, and at least one person will show up. Next time, it won't be your first show and you'll still be nervous, but now you'll be nervous and experienced!

WHERE WILL YOU SHOW?

Everywhere you can! When you're first starting out, you need to show your work often and build up your artist résumé. While you are in high school or college, there will be exhibition opportunities through your art program. But don't stop there. Look for places on and off campus where you and your friends can set up a show together. Don't forget to document what you do in writing and in photos for your résumé, website, and social media, for example.

Take advantage of every exhibition opportunity that comes your way (with a few exceptions—see the sidebar "Red Flags"), bearing in mind that as your career advances, you'll be able to focus on only the better opportunities.

Check out the "Art Exhibition Venues" sidebar for a wide variety of spaces that show art. Some may surprise you!

ART EXHIBITION VENUES

An art venue is any place that exhibits art. Here is a small sampling of the kinds of venues that exist. Depending on your goals, one venue or another might be at the top of your personal priorities list.

- Art centers
- Srt fairs/festivals
- Art school galleries
- Churches, synagogues, or other religious spaces
- College/university art galleries
- College/university community spaces
- Commercial galleries
- Community/nonprofit galleries
- Concert/performing arts halls and lobbies
- Corporate offices/lobbies
- Group artist studio buildings
- Hospitals
- International museums
- Juried exhibitions
- Local businesses
- Local museums
- National museums
- Pop-ups
- Private museums
- Private school galleries
- Public libraries
- Public museums

Commercial Galleries

Having a gallery—preferably in New York City—that represents your work, gives you solo exhibitions, includes you in group exhibitions, and sells your work at high prices to eager collectors (while assuming all the costs for promoting your work) is the ultimate goal for many artists. But only a handful of artists achieve this status.

Gallery representation means that somebody who commands respect in the art world sees value in your work and believes their collectors will want to own it. Artists with a gallery can usually expect to be included in group shows, receive a solo exhibition every few years, and be considered for inclusion in the gallery's booth at major art fairs. If a gallery sells your artwork, it is normal for them to keep 50 percent of the price as their sales commission.

Get to know your own art community by visiting galleries and getting to know gallerists, art dealers, and the artists who show with them. Make appointments to show them your work, if you can. Remember that the best way to get a gallery's attention is the recommendation of another artist who shows with them.

Galleries open frequently and disappear frequently—sometimes taking artists' work and unpaid money with them. More and more, galleries are shifting costs to the artist. As Caroll Michels says in *How to Survive and Prosper as an Artist*, "The exaltation of gallery status can quickly dissipate when one discovers exactly what being a gallery artist entails."[3]

If you don't have a commercial gallery, don't let that stop you or even slow you down. There are so many ways to grow your list of followers, cultivate relationships with collectors, and show your work in other venues that many artists today do not even want a gallery! Some artists get together and start their own gallery. It's important to be ready to create your own opportunities before, during, or after gallery representation comes along or instead of any gallery representation at all.

For a great introduction to presenting your work to galleries, read *I'd Rather Be in the Studio! The Artist's No-Excuse Guide to Self-Promotion* by Alyson B. Stanfield (see Further Resources on page 119).

Nonprofit Galleries

Nonprofit galleries, such as university or community galleries, exist to show artwork for reasons other than sales: to enhance educational programming, to support a political or social concept, or to present artwork because of its own merit, for example.

Nonprofit galleries can be an excellent choice for artists who make conceptual, installation, performance, or ephemeral work that is not designed or intended to be sold in commercial galleries. If your artwork falls into one of these categories, consider approaching nonprofit galleries such as college and university galleries, art centers, or museums with an exhibition proposal.

Grants are often used to fund these types of exhibitions and can be granted either directly to the artist or to the organization. Writing a grant proposal is an art in itself. See Further Resources on good places to start learning about the grant-writing process.

"Landing a grant requires work, and that work usually involves writing a proposal or grant application. In your proposal, you have to explain why you want the money, why the granting organization should support the project, and how you intend to spend the funds. You are expected to include a detailed budget and samples of your work. Your application is judged by a panel of your peers—that means other artists—in a competitive process."[4]—Gigi Rosenberg

Juried Shows

Juried exhibitions let you exhibit your work and build your artist's résumé, especially if you want to show in places far from where you live. There are some things to know about entering juried shows.

- **Cost:** There is usually an entry fee, currently between $25 and $35. Shipping your work to and from a juried exhibition can also be expensive. Plan to budget a limited amount annually for juried shows to help you be selective about which ones you enter.
- **Presentation matters:** It's important to have high-quality images of your work that show it to its best advantage.
- **Follow the rules:** Read the prospectus and follow it to the letter. If they want images no larger than 1,500 pixels on the longest side, don't send them images larger than that. If they only want photography, don't send them paintings.
- **You're not in until you're in:** No matter how well you think your work matches what the show has asked for, you might not get in. But that's no reflection on you or your work. Many more artists enter juried shows than will fit in the space. The juror is trying to pick art that works together in a coherent way or makes a specific statement. If you don't get into a juried show, don't worry about it. It's just a choice made by one person on one day for reasons you know nothing about.

RED FLAGS

Unfortunately, there are all too many people out there who try to take advantage of artists. Some may believe they are "helping" artists and making a living at the same time. Others are running outright scams. Here are some red flags to watch out for.

- Juried shows with high fees. If a show charges more than $35 for an entry fee, think twice. A show in a truly great location might charge around $40 for three images, but if you see fees of $50 or more, or fees for a single image with additional charges for more images, you should probably skip the show.
- Commercial galleries that offer a new juried show every month. If a commercial gallery is making its rent through fees from juried shows rather than sales, it doesn't have much incentive to promote or sell artwork.
- Email scams. One classic scam is a would-be husband looking for a gift for his wife or someone who claims to be redecorating a new home or business in a foreign country. They might name a particular piece. Later the scammers send a check for more than the price of the piece and ask the artist to send a wire transfer back for the difference. When the check bounces, the artist is out the amount of the wire transfer and often the piece as well. Email scams change all the time, so be on your guard.
- Commercial galleries that don't pay. This is, sadly, a common problem with certain commercial galleries. The gallery accepts an artist's work, sells it, and doesn't pay the commission. Sometimes the artist doesn't know the piece has sold until they ask for it back. The usual excuse is that the gallery had to pay its expenses first, like rent, light, and heating. But those expenses are not the artist's responsibility. If a gallery uses your money to pay its rent, that's stealing. Ask other artists about their experiences with a particular gallery before signing a contract.

Small Group Shows

If a commercial or nonprofit gallery is putting together a curated show and invites you to be in it, what should you do? (Hint: say yes.) These kinds of curated, small-group shows are considered more prestigious than larger juried shows.

You can also create your own small-group shows by working with two to four other artists whose art "works and plays well" with yours. You can plan your show around things your work has in common, a social or political idea, formal elements, or something similar about who you are as people, like a shared background. Go back to the "Art Exhibition Venues" sidebar to get some ideas about where you could have your show.

Open Studios

"An open studio provides you with an amazing opportunity to create relationships with potential collectors. . . . The goal is not only to give visitors an experience to remember, it's to give you long-standing relationships with buyers and potential buyers."[5]—Jason Horejs

Artists who have studios in the same building or work in their city's arts district often plan to open their studios to the public at the same time. This can be an evening event or a weekend afternoon. If there is a regular open studio event in your area, sign up for it. If there isn't, consider working with other artists whose studios are physically close to yours to set up an open studio event. When these events are held regularly (the first Friday of the month, for instance) and you work hard to get the word out through your e-newsletter, press releases, and so forth, you can build up a regular following of art lovers who will come every time to see your latest work.

You can also hold an open studio event on your own. You'll have to do all the planning and organization by yourself, but visitors will be focused on your work and yours alone.

See Further Resources for great tips on how to hold an open studio event.

EXHIBITION PROPOSALS

Exhibition proposals are used to suggest an exhibition to a venue. The most important rule is to *follow the venue's directions*. Some venues want everything emailed through an online portal on their website. Some want you to use an online service like www.submittable.com. Some want you to mail a CD or DVD. Some want a physical proposal, printed on paper, with perfect photos of your artwork, all presented in a lovely folder.

What goes in your proposal? Usually

- a one-page description of the proposed exhibition, including a statement describing what the exhibition is about and why it would be a good fit for that venue;
- a works list that matches the images being submitted—make sure you know what information the venue wants on the works list (e.g., title, medium, size, year, price);
- your most up-to-date artist resume or CV;
- images of your works, ten–twenty, in focus, with correct color and no hotspots or shadows. Follow the venue's directions for size and resolution of digital images. If sending printed images, make sure they look good and represent your work well.

You might also include

- reviews, interviews, exhibition catalogs, or other information that shows what you have already done;
- letters of support from art-world figures (local, regional, or national) who can speak to your professionalism and the importance of your artwork.

Art Fairs and Festivals

There are three different kinds of art fairs, and it is important to understand the difference.

International Art Fairs. The Venice Biennale, Art Basel, the Frieze Art Fair, Art Miami—these are some of the biggest, most prestigious places where art is shown. Top art galleries from around the world rent space in one massive location, highlighting only their top artists. Only commercial galleries may participate in this kind of art fair. Art dealers, art buyers, major collectors, and other visitors travel from all over the world to attend the big art fairs. Some fairs, like Art Basel, happen every year. Others, called "biennials," happen every other year.

There are different art fairs for different segments of the art world, but they are all opportunities for artists to share their work with potential collectors.

Showing at a big, international art fair is one of the largest parts of a gallery's budget—it is a major investment, a major undertaking, and a major financial risk. A booth at Art Basel, for instance, can be as much as $400,000—then there are the costs of shipping, travel, lodging, and so forth. Galleries must be confident that the expense will be worth it in terms of sales and recognition over the next year.

Artists' Art Fairs.   In recent years, a new kind of art fair has sprung up. Events like the Affordable Art Fair (e.g., in London, New York, and Chicago) give smaller galleries, dealers, and art collectives the chance to show their artists' work in a fair environment but at a lower cost. Some fairs will accept applications from individual artists. Other fairs recruit individual artists, such as the stARTup Art Fair (e.g., in San Francisco, Los Angeles, and Houston), or The Other Art Fair (e.g., in Brooklyn, London, and Sydney). Work must be juried into the show, and visitors can buy work directly from the exhibitors.

These fairs are expensive, but not as expensive as the big, international art fairs. For instance, in 2018, booth fees for the Affordable Art Fair in New York City ranged from $5,500 to $20,800 depending on both size and location. StARTup Art Fair says booth fees "begin" at $2,000. The Other Art Fair booth fees are under $1,800. In addition, there are shipping, storage, travel, and other expenses. Before participating in these kinds of fairs, think long and hard about expense versus results.

Outdoor Art Fairs/Festivals.   These are the kinds of art fairs that you see in local parks or other community spaces. Artists and craftspeople display their wares at booths, talk to visitors, and sell art directly to the public. Some of these fairs are juried and some are open (meaning that anyone who pays the booth fee may exhibit).

Booth fees are much lower for outdoor art festivals. The Mystic Outdoor Art Festival in Mystic, Connecticut, for instance, charges $350–$750 for a booth, plus a jurying fee. If you participate in an art festival away from your hometown, there will also be travel, storage, lodging, and other expenses to take into account.

There is a prejudice among some people in the art world against showing at local art fairs and festivals: they assume that there is a difference between a "gallery artist" and an "art festival artist" and that one artist cannot and should not be both. Many artists make the kind of art that will sell well at an outdoor art fair or festival but wouldn't do as well in a traditional commercial gallery space. You'll have to decide for yourself what you think about that.

Commissions and Public Art

Artists can be paid for creating work for a specific purpose. Sometimes that involves a commission from a client to create an artwork they ask for. Other times, it can involve working with a community to create a piece of art for the benefit of all.

Commissions are a way to make art in collaboration with a public project or a private collector.

WORKING ON COMMISSION

"Being asked to do a commission can be very flattering. It means someone likes your work enough to buy something from you before they've even seen it. . . . Working on a commission can be rewarding, in that the collector's priorities challenge you to experiment in new directions."[6]—Heather Darcy Bhandari and Jonathan Melber

You might make art on commission regularly (e.g., portraits) or only once in a while. Working on commission is different from making art on your own. It's a partnership with the commissioning patron, and good communication and clear expectations (in writing) are very important to making that partnership work.

If you think you might ever work on commission, check out the Further Resources for some great information on how to make this a good experience for everyone involved.

PUBLIC ART

Public art projects give artists a chance to be recognized as important contributors and to be paid reasonably for their artwork. It's also an opportunity to work with your community—kids and adults—on something that will be part of that community for years to come. Public art projects create a sense of belonging and value, reinforce civic and cultural pride, and improve public health by reducing stress and improving mood. Public art gives artists a chance to create something noteworthy and gives nonartists the chance to learn about art making, history, culture, place, and much more.

Public art projects can be looking for almost any kind of artwork—2-D, 3-D, indoor, outdoor, permanent, or removable, for example. Artists who focus on public art learn the ins and outs of how to be chosen for these paying projects.

Among the U.S. states and territories, twenty-eight fund public art specifically. In percent-for-art programs, a certain percentage of money—usually about 1 percent of the budget—is designated for art purchases or commissions when public buildings are being built or renovated. The state art agency will put out a request for proposal (RFP) with all the parameters involved, such as the size and location of the building. Sometimes the agency will offer a tour of the location for interested artists. Usually states will accept proposals from out-of-state artists but will tend to give preference to in-state artists. Depending on the project, artists may submit plans for a unique work created for the space. Other times, artists may submit an existing work that fits the requirements of the RFP.

Some states also purchase existing work directly from artists for a state arts bank. These are works of art that can be displayed in existing public buildings—for example, in offices, lobbies, conference rooms, or hallways.

- Alaska—Percent for Art
- Colorado—Art in Public Places
- Connecticut—Art in Public Spaces
- District of Columbia—DC Creates!
- Florida—Art in State Buildings
- Guam—Art in Public Places
- Hawaii—Art in Public Places
- Illinois—Art-in-Architecture
- Iowa—Art in State Buildings
- Louisiana—Percent for Art
- Maine—Public Art
- Maryland—Commission on Public Art
- Massachusetts—Percent for Art
- Minnesota—Percent for Art in Public Places
- Montana—Percent for Art
- Nebraska—Percent for Art
- New Hampshire—Percent for Art
- New Jersey—Arts Inclusion
- New Mexico—Art in Public Places
- Ohio—Percent for Art
- Oklahoma—Art in Public Places
- Oregon—Public Art
- Rhode Island—Public Art
- South Carolina—Percent for Art
- Texas—Public Art
- Utah—Public Art
- Vermont—Art in State Buildings
- Washington—Art in Public Places
- Wyoming—Art in Public Buildings

Commercial Artist Jobs

Artists are employed by companies or industries in many roles—as employees or as freelancers—to create visual art in support of their employer's or client's goals rather than for their own self-expression. A job in commercial art can be rewarding in and of itself, or it can be a way to support your personal artwork.

Andrew Gordon of Pixar offers some advice for people who want to be animators. His insights are true of any of the commercial art fields:

Firstly, build a really strong foundation of traditional art because even though you don't have to learn it, it helps in the design of poses, in the staging of shots, etc. . . .

Really sink yourself into your work and just be dedicated to it and focus on an aspect of it that you like. If you want to be a lighter, go into lighting. If you like animation, focus on animations and not so much on lighting. Really go deep in your understanding of your profession.

At some point you want to be able to have the chops to do other things, whether it be directing or doing a short. I think that doing films or pieces of work that show storytelling ultimately helps in the very end or during your career because the medium is all about telling stories.[7]

Commercial art jobs let you use your creativity and artistic skills to support yourself.

YOUR COMMERCIAL ART PORTFOLIO

Commercial art jobs are "portfolio-driven" rather than "degree-driven," which means that potential employers want to see what you can do and what computer and other skills you have. If you have a good portfolio and know how to work the relevant programs, you can apply for most of these kinds of jobs no matter what your degree is in.

1. Maintain your portfolio in print and online. Catch an employer's eye by including a link to your online portfolio in your résumé or application. Bring your book portfolio to the interview.

2. Only include your best work. If you have doubts about a particular piece, so will a potential employer. If it's good, include it. If it isn't, leave it out.

3. Include a range of your best work. Demonstrate drawing, photography, digital art, and layout skills. Organize these in both your print and online portfolios to make the different types of work easy to find, and include a table of contents.

4. Keep it up to date. Your portfolio should always have your most current, best work front and center. When you finish something that's portfolio worthy, put it in your portfolio! (The same goes for your résumé, by the way.)

5. Provide context. For each piece, provide a short, written description of the purpose of the piece and a little something about the decisions you made to meet the requirements. For digital work, add a note about which programs you used to create the piece.

6. Start strong, end strong. Your strongest pieces should be at the beginning and at the end of your portfolio. You need to make a good first impression to keep them looking at your work, and you need to make a good last impression because people remember how things end better than how they start.

ART DIRECTOR

Art directors are responsible for the visual style of a final product, like a movie or a magazine. The art director creates the overall design of the project and is in charge of a team that develops the artwork. Art directors usually work their way up from other positions as artists, graphic designers, illustrators, photographers, copy editors, or similar jobs.

- The median salary for art directors is about $93,000 per year.
- The U.S. Bureau of Labor Statistics (BLS) predicts job growth of 5 percent between 2016 and 2026, but this is also a highly competitive field.
- Art directors hold bachelor's or master's degrees in art or design and have significant previous experience.
- Some of the qualities art directors need are creativity, good leadership, time-management and communication skills, and resourcefulness and adaptability.

CONCEPT ARTIST

Concept artists work with the visual side of a game or animated movie: the overall style, backgrounds and locations, characters, and props. Concept artists work with directors, project managers, or architects to interpret and realize their ideas. A concept artist's portfolio should show imaginative and well-executed characters, creatures, costumes, props, interior and exterior environments, vehicles, and technology. Companies also like to see your personal artwork, sketches, and figure drawing studies. Concept art is a highly competitive field, so applicants need to show their absolutely best work.

- Pay varies with the size and success of the game company, but median annual pay is around $55,000.
- The BLS predicts job growth of about 2 percent over ten years.
- Concept artists usually have bachelor's degrees.
- Some of the qualities concept artists need are strong artistic, technical, and communication skills and the ability to function well in a team environment.

Character and concept artists imagine and create the world of games, movies, and more.

CHARACTER ARTIST

Character artists work as part of a team to develop the look and attributes of characters in a game to coordinate with story line, game concept, and other characters. Character artists design the characters, which then go to the animators to be realized. Character artists need to show mastery in drawing, anatomy, drapery, proportion, and perspective. A character artist's portfolio should include sketches and completed images of a wide variety of imaginative characters, each shown from different angles and in different positions.

- Pay varies with the size and success of the game company, but median annual pay is around $43,000.
- The BLS predicts job growth of about 8 percent between 2016 and 2026.
- Character artists usually have bachelor's degrees.
- Some of the qualities character artists need are strong artistic, technical, and communication skills and the ability function well in a team environment.

GRAPHIC DESIGNER

Graphic designers create web pages, logos, book and magazine covers and interiors, ads, and other marketing materials. Graphic designers need to know design principles, computer design programs, and printing. Most graphic designers use computer programs like those in Adobe Creative Suite. Graphic designers work as part of the communications team in businesses and nonprofit organizations or as independent freelancers for multiple clients.

- Median annual pay is around $49,000.
- The BLS predicts the field will grow by about 4 percent between 2016 and 2026.
- Most graphic designers have bachelor's degrees and many have BFA degrees in art or design.
- Some of the qualities graphic designers need are time management skills, people skills, verbal and written communication skills, and artistic creativity.

ILLUSTRATOR

Illustrators are often freelancers who work with client publishing companies to create illustrations for children's books, book covers, technical instructions, coloring books, and other products. Illustrators do not typically work directly with authors but sometimes create their own children's books as author-illustrators. Illustrators need to have mastery in drawing (especially drawing children), anatomy, drapery, proportion, and perspective as well as imagination and creativity.

- Median annual illustrator salary is about $49,500, with entry-level illustrators making as little as $21,600 and the most experienced, well-known illustrators making over $100,000.
- The BLS predicts about 7 percent job growth between 2016 and 2026.
- Some illustrators hold BFAs, while others develop their portfolios without a degree or with a degree in a different field.
- Some of the qualities illustrators need are time management skills, people skills, verbal and written communication skills, and artistic creativity.

MEDICAL ILLUSTRATOR/ANIMATOR

According to ExploreHealthCareers.org (https://explorehealthcareers.org), medical illustrators/animators "create imagery that advances medical science knowledge and empowers health literacy for patients and the public. They have the medical and scientific knowledge to grasp complex information, distil it down and communicate the story in a clear visual narrative that is accurate, educational and engaging." To learn more about this specialized career field, visit the Association of Medical Illustrators website at www.ami.org.

- Median salary for medical illustrator/animators is $62,000. Supervisors and creative directors average closer to $85,000.
- There are not as many medical illustrator/animators as are needed, so job prospects in this field are excellent.
- Most have master's degrees and have studied interdisciplinary science. Courses can include anatomy, pathology, microanatomy, physiology, embryology, neuroanatomy, surgical illustration, color theory, instructional design, photography, interactive media development, and 3-D

modeling and web design, plus traditional drawing and computer applications.

- Some of the qualities needed by medical illustrator/animators are artistic, technical, and anatomical knowledge.

Art World Careers

There are many careers in the world of galleries, museums, and auction houses. Fine artists can work their way up from entry-level to upper-level in these careers or they can stay in school for a master's degree in art or art history to get ready to work in these settings. To learn more, see "Art Museum Job Profiles" at www.thebalancecareers.com/art-museum-career-profiles-4161775.

Artists who teach share their love of art and their creative skills with others.

ARTS EDUCATION COORDINATOR

Arts education coordinators work for museums, community art centers, and nonprofit galleries. They hire teachers, schedule classes, train volunteers, set up exhibitions of student work, and maintain records. Experience teaching art or working in another role (paid or volunteer) at an art institution is an important qualification.

- Median annual salary is about $35,400.
- As with other museum jobs, the BLS predicts growth of 11 to 14 percent by 2026.
- A bachelor's degree is usually required along with experience in education, communication, art, and marketing.
- Some of the qualities needed for arts education coordinators are people skills and organizational and communication skills.

ART HANDLER

Art handlers work for a museum, auction house, or gallery. They are responsible for the physical, hands-on work of packing, crating, moving, and storing art and artifacts.

- Average salary is around $30,000 per year, with salaries at New York auction houses being higher.
- Art handlers do not need a college degree.
- Some of the qualities needed for art handlers are physical strength, basic carpentry skills, and carefulness, plus a valid driver's license and knowledge of tools.

CURATORIAL ASSISTANT

Curatorial assistants work directly with curators or associate curators to do collection research and prepare exhibitions. The job can involve communicating with artists, maintaining records, and working on exhibition catalogs. Experience is important, so look for internships and student jobs in the field while you're still in college.

- Median salary is about $40,000 per year.
- The BLS predicts job growth of 14 percent through 2026.
- Education required is usually a bachelor's or master's degree in art, art history, or museum studies.
- Some of the qualities needed for curatorial assistants are good interpersonal skills and good communications and technical skills.

CURATORIAL TECHNICIAN

A curatorial technician (also called "registrar") for an art museum works behind the scenes to help take care of the artwork and to install/de-install exhibitions. They may help with research, inventory, and cataloging or with educational programming. These jobs can be full-time or part-time and may require evening and weekend work. Volunteering or interning at a museum is a good way to gain experience and recommendations.

- Median salary is about $48,400, although pay varies in different locations.
- The BLS predicts about 13 percent growth in this field between 2016 and 2026.
- Curatorial technician jobs don't require a degree, but advancement usually does. Most curatorial technicians learn important skills (like how to handle artwork appropriately) on the job.
- Some of the qualities needed for curatorial technicians are detail orientation, good hand-eye coordination, and physical strength and stamina. Often a valid driver's license is required.

GALLERY ASSISTANT

An art gallery assistant helps the gallery director, especially with the business side of running a commercial art gallery, doing things like greeting visitors, maintaining a website and mailing list, dealing with paperwork and phone calls, shipping and handling art work, and communicating with artists and collectors. This is one job where appearance matters: the gallery assistant must dress well and be impeccably groomed. Art gallery assistants work full- or part-time and some evenings and weekends. Competition for art gallery assistant jobs is high. Prior experience (paid or volunteer) is important, so seek internship opportunities while you're still in school.

- Median salary is about $42,000.
- A bachelor's degree in art or art history is required and sometimes a master's degree, depending on the gallery. Prior work experience can make up for a shortfall in educational requirements.
- Some of the qualities needed for gallery assistants are good organizational, communication, and social media skills; an ability to focus on

long- and short-term projects; self-motivation; and a willingness to take the initiative.

MUSEUM ATTENDANT

An art museum attendant welcomes visitors and helps them find their way around while protecting the art by making sure visitors follow the institution's rules (e.g., no photography, no food or drink, no touching the art). The job combines customer service with security. Artists with or without college degrees may like this work—you spend your whole day surrounded by art!

- The average salary is around $35,000 depending on location and experience.
- The BLS predicts museum jobs will grow about 11 percent by 2026.
- No college degree is required to be an art museum attendant.
- Some of the qualities needed for museum attendants include good people skills and communication and observational skills.

STUDIO ASSISTANT

Usually hired by busy, established artists, art studio assistants handle daily studio and business tasks—anything from running errands to stretching canvases to bookkeeping to helping fabricate large pieces. Studio assistants often work part time in the established artist's studio or home. Salaries are low because part of a studio assistant's compensation is being mentored by the established artist and being introduced to the art community. These jobs are usually found through word-of-mouth or personal recommendations.

- The average pay is $10 to $12 per hour but an experienced, long-term studio assistant can make as much as $40,000 per year.
- Art studio assistants are usually still in art school or are recent graduates.
- Some of the qualities needed for studio assistants are a good attitude, a willingness to work hard, computer skills, good people or customer service skills, and usually some expertise in the artist's medium (painters need painters for studio assistants, sculptors need sculptors, photographers need photographers, etc.).

Acting on Your Plan

Now that you have an idea of what's out there in terms of careers for fine artists, let's take a look at how to act on your plan. Chapter 3 is all about the education path.

ANDY MOERLEIN—SCULPTOR

Sculptor Andy Moerlein in the studio. Photo by Donna Dodson.

Andy Moerlein is a sculptor based in Massachusetts. He holds a bachelor's degree in visual art from Dartmouth College and an MFA in sculpture from Cornell University. He has taught at the high-school level at Derryfield School and Hampstead Academy, both in New Hampshire. In addition to making his own sculpture, Andy and his wife, sculptor Donna Dodson, work as a collaborative team called Myth Makers to create sculptures different from what either makes on their own.

What kind of art do you make?

I am primarily a sculptor. I am an eclectic materialist and a passionate patron of the arts. Museums and galleries are my favorite form of entertainment, and my art making reflects the intersection of arts that I see—historic, contemporary, and commercial in equal quantities. I am never singularly wed to a medium but rather see traditional bronze, clay, and wood as equal to performance, video, and industrial fabrication. Concept, materials, and craft collude with ideas and lead me to my expressive destination and final product: art.

How long have you been an artist?

I have always been accused of being an outlander in my approach to interpreting and reacting to the world. I was given an introduction to fine art when working in the wood shop in college and have been thinking of myself as an artist ever since.

Did you always intend to be an artist or did it happen later?

I was a maker and builder of fine but unexpected furniture and homes, and a sideways thinker/inventor/tinkerer/designer all of my remembered life. Calling what I did "art" was not in my family or home vocabulary, so it was college that brought that possibility to my attention.

How did you learn your art?

I went to college and saw many amazing artists in the studios, gallery talks, and shows. I observed how great artists researched. The example was accidental and not class-related. I practiced techniques and materials in classes. I am mentored by life. I follow many fine artists, do studio visits constantly, travel to museums and galleries like an addiction.

How did (or didn't) your education prepare you for the different aspects of the job of artist?

I got no training in the business of being an artist. That has come in slow stages—all hard earned. An MBA might be of more benefit to an artist than an MFA.

What other jobs do you/did you do in addition to being an artist?

I am lately rather busy as an artist, touring shows and doing talks/lectures and workshops. I am and have always been a teacher/educator, when it does not conflict my show calendar. I love the lively society of the classroom.

What's the best part of being an artist?

I so live for the long hours of creating. I love to work. My family were agrarian-based Midwesterners and they raised me to work. It is in my blood. Art is work. As an artist I also appreciate the generous invitation into other artists' lives. My colleagues and peers enrich my life constantly.

What's the worst part of being an artist?

The meager support for midcareer artists.

What's the most surprising thing about being an artist?

That I never get tired when I am working. It makes me stronger and happier than any sport or challenge I have ever engaged in.

What advice would you give a young person who wants to be an artist?

Practice every day. If you cannot work daily, you probably do not need to be an artist. Perhaps you should buy art?

Pursuing the Education Path

Do Artists Need to Study Art?

*A*bsolutely—artists need to study art. For artists, learning is a lifelong process. Artists need to study technique, art history, art criticism, and what other artists are doing, in addition to developing their own artwork. But does that necessarily mean getting a bachelor of fine arts (BFA) degree?

Fine artists are always learning.

Art school gives you a complete background in art methods, studio practice, and art history and lets you begin building art relationships.

"Studying art will help you discern the message you want to convey with your work. Analyze the ways other artists make statements with their work, and determine which methods you find most effective. The more experiences you have with art, the more widespread your inspiration for your next project."[1]—Mary Hilliard

A BFA from an art school or through a college or university is considered the professional art degree at the undergraduate level. In general, artists frequently follow the BFA with a master of fine arts (MFA), which is the "terminal degree" in visual art. That means an MFA is equivalent to a doctorate in another field, and someone with an MFA is qualified to teach at the college or university level.

"Art school gives creative thinkers the space to explore, experiment and develop their own unique vision; ultimately, it gives artists and designers the chance to think and act in radical new ways that can influence the way we see the world."[2]—Nigel Carrington, vice-chancellor, University of the Arts, London

Pros and Cons of a BFA

PROS

1. Working toward a BFA provides (or should provide) a coherent introduction to a variety of media with an opportunity to delve more deeply into them; an overview of art history to help you find your place and understand the work of those who came before you; an introduction to the concepts and process of critique; and several years of focusing on your artwork. Ideally, an art school or university art program should also give you some idea of the business of art and help you begin building relationships in the art world.
2. Working toward a BFA will give you a very specific focus on art throughout your higher education experience.
3. Art school gives you the opportunity to spend your time immersed in art, talking about art with other artists, finding your media, and developing your own style.
4. If your university also offers a BA in art, you can combine your art major with a broader liberal arts background.
5. A BFA from a college or university costs about the same as any other degree from the same institution.

CONS

1. Depending on where you go to school, a BFA can be very expensive. Some of the top private art schools in the country also have some of the highest tuitions. Even with scholarships and grants, the cost of these schools can result in the kind of debt that most professional artists would have difficulty paying off over a lifetime.
2. Because the BFA is considered a professional degree rather than a liberal arts degree, you will have less time to learn about a broad range of subjects.
3. Art supplies are quite expensive. Be prepared to devote a large portion of your school budget to purchasing art supplies.
4. Although the BFA is considered a professional degree, you might not be introduced to any or enough art business information to begin a career as an artist right out of school (see chapter 4).

It is certainly possible to begin and maintain a career in visual art without a BFA. There are many artists who learn from professional artists by taking classes at local art centers, through community education programs, or through individual study. Some people major in another subject in college and then decide to begin making art alongside another career or make a career switch to fine art later on. "Outsider artists" are those from communities that are underrepresented in the art world or in society at large. Many of these artists are genuinely self-taught.

In art school or on your own time, learning art involves exploration and discovery by making art and making more art.

Pros and Cons of Non-BFA Options

PROS

1. Throughout history, most artists did not go to art school. Traditionally, artists learned from masters by working with them in their studios. Anyone can learn art techniques by taking classes with professional, working artists individually, at local art centers, or in community education programs run by community colleges, colleges, and universities.

2. You can pursue another degree in college or the university that will provide you with a broader education or prepare you for another career. Art teachers usually earn degrees in art education. Art therapists combine art and psychology. You might want to study science or foreign languages or history—all of these subjects will feed your art practice.

3. Holding a different bachelor's degree will not keep you out of an MFA program if you want to pursue one later on. Your portfolio and recommendations will count most.

4. If you finish college with a different degree and *then* decide you want to be an artist, you will have access to classes, professional artists, videos, art organizations, and everything else you need to learn and progress in your art.

CONS

1. While your portfolio is your primary way of introducing yourself in the art world, having a BFA shows your dedication to the field. In some cases, a BFA puts you a step ahead of your competition.

2. Many upscale galleries will only consider artists who hold an MFA unless the artist falls into the category of outsider artist. It is much easier to go directly into an MFA program immediately following a BFA than with another degree because you will already have a portfolio, a solid art history background, recommendations, and a familiarity with the norms and customs of an art school or art department.

Whether you go to art school or not, as an artist you not only must continue learning about art all your life, *you will want to*. First and foremost, that means learning by doing—creating, more creating, discarding unsuccessful work and keeping successful work, and then more creating. Learn new techniques or approaches by taking classes. Follow artists you like on social media. Watch YouTube videos to see how different artists approach their work or pick up new techniques that enhance the kind of work you do. Read books on art history and journals on contemporary art. Go to galleries and museums and get to know other artists, gallerists, arts administrators, and collectors.

One of the best ways to continue to expand your horizons is by looking at artwork that comes from a completely different perspective than yours. Do you carve wooden horses that embody the cowboy experience? Go to a contemporary art museum and look closely at abstract paintings or lithographs. Figure out what those artists are doing and how it relates to what you're trying to do. Likewise, if you make avant-garde installations that incorporate video and movement to create discomfort in viewers about socially relevant topics, take a long look at Michelangelo's sculptures. What do you see? What would it feel like to make that work? How does it connect to what you're doing?

Before Art School

How do you prepare yourself to become an artist? Before you begin art school, experience all the art you can. Take classes, go to exhibits, travel to museums, look at art books, read about artists who interest you in books and online, and even scroll through Instagram.

LEARN ART

While you're still in high school, take all the art classes you can. Whatever your school offers, take it. Get to know your art teachers and ask them for feedback on your work. How can you make it better? Are there any common mistakes you're making that you could fix? Do they notice anything about the work that makes it special? Even if a particular teacher doesn't have good answers to these questions, it's good to get in the mind-set of asking them. Be respectful and polite, and consider what you're being told even if it doesn't make sense to you at the time. It might become clear later on. Also, your school art teachers are the first people you'll want to ask for art school recommendations.

If you don't have access to art classes in school, seek out community art classes. These are usually taught by professional artists who know a lot about their own medium. This is an opportunity to take classes that aren't offered at your school or to go deeper in a medium that speaks to you (painting, drawing, ceramics, paper-making, etc.)

Many high schools offer classes like

- ceramics
- drawing

- graphic design
- painting
- photography
- sculpture

Community art classes are often offered by local nonprofit arts centers in afterschool programs or summer camps. Sometimes professional artists will offer classes in their own studios to individual students or small groups. Classes will vary based on which artists are available to teach and what they do, but they often include things like

- beginning and advanced acrylic painting
- beginning and advanced drawing
- beginning and advanced oil painting
- digital photography
- eco-art
- sculpture
- therapeutic creative expression
- video and film

SEE ART

The best way to see good art is in person. So go where it is. If you are lucky enough to have a local art museum or two, go again and again. Look at all the collections—even if you're not sure what the appeal is—and spend some time with your favorite pieces. Go to every traveling exhibit that comes through town. Go to art shows in galleries and nonprofit spaces to see the work of your fellow local artists.

Make an effort to travel to other places and see galleries and museums wherever you go. Sometimes it just costs too much to go somewhere else, even for a short period of time, but look for low-cost opportunities to visit places with great art to see.

Don't forget to take some breaks. Artists often get "art overload" in museums from the massive influx of visual information. Remember to give your brain a chance to process all the art you're seeing. It might take several visits to see everything a large museum has to offer.

MAKE ART

You do this already, right? Or you wouldn't be wondering if an art degree is right for you. So keep it up! Don't limit yourself to class assignments. Make what *you* want to make too.

Keep a sketchbook. It's a great place to make those all-important observational drawings as well as for planning your personal work and making notes on art that occurs to you. Keep your sketchbook with you so that you can use it whenever inspiration strikes.

The work you do before applying to art school will make up the portfolio you use to apply. Keep track of all your best pieces and be sure you have excellent digital images of them made.

Applying to Art School

> "It's necessary to find out the key traits and criteria important to the schools you're applying to. Find this out early in the admissions process and give yourself plenty of time to prepare. Convey the four P's; passion, preparation, portfolio, and passion and you'll make the admission staff's selection process easy!"[3]—Christina Macres

In addition to all the usual things you need to do to get ready to apply to college, there are some other things you need to do that are specific to applying for art school.

FIND THE RIGHT FIT

It is more important to attend the school that is the right fit for you than one with a big name, especially at the bachelor's degree level. Would you feel more comfortable at a large school or a small one? Closer to home or closer to a major art center? Remember, an art department within a large university can be like a small art school in terms of what you can study and the opportunities to meet like-minded people.

The best art schools and college or university art departments are highly competitive. It's important to know what these schools are like; what they focus on; what kind of work their faculty, students, and graduate students do; and what they're looking for in prospective students.

Go to each school's website and see what they are asking for in your application. If they want examples of specific exercises, be sure to include your best examples in the portfolio you submit to them. Art schools use their own admissions criteria, but in general, you can expect that they'll require

- a description of your educational background
- letters of recommendation
- an admissions essay
- an interview
- a portfolio

> "School visits and portfolio reviews will help you take the next step in your application process, but also give you name recognition when it comes time to actually evaluate your application for admission. Not to mention, visiting the school will give you the chance to talk to current students about why they chose this particular college, and you can check out the sort of work they're creating."[4]—Mary Hilliard

Accreditation

Before applying to any college or university, be sure that it holds the right accreditation. While it might seem like national accreditation is better than regional accreditation, the opposite is actually true. According to EDSmart:

> Regional accreditation is older and more prestigious that national, except in a few cases. Most non-profit colleges have regional accreditation, not national accreditation. . . . regional accrediting organizations operate in specific regions of the country. These organizations grant accreditation to schools, colleges, and universities showing that their credits and degrees meet minimum standards. This is a voluntary process that self-regulates the higher education industry.

> Regionally accredited colleges are mostly academically-oriented, non-profit or state-owned institutions. Regionally accredited institutions are reluctant to accept transfer credits from nationally accredited institutions, mainly because the latter hasn't met the stringent standards of faculty qualifications and library resources.[5]

In addition to institutional accreditation, you should also look for programs that are accredited by their appropriate organization. For instance, the National Association of Schools of Art and Design (NASAD) is the leading accrediting body for art and design programs. This kind of accreditation is not required and some schools don't choose to have their programs accredited, but in general, accreditation gives a "seal of approval" that tells you the program meets certain standards.

PORTFOLIO

Your portfolio is a showcase of all your best work. At different times in your life, it will contain different types or groupings of work, depending on what you're using it for. When you are applying to art school, your portfolio should be a broad representation of your best artwork in the various media you use plus observational drawing. (Wait—didn't we already talk about observational drawing in chapter 1? Yes, we did—and now we're talking about it again. Why? Check out the sidebar "National Portfolio Day.")

Your portfolio contains examples of your best work—and it changes to reflect your growth as an artist.

What Should Your Portfolio Contain?

Different schools will have different requirements, but in general you want to showcase

- ten to twenty examples of your absolute best work (ten great pieces are better than twenty mediocre ones)
- the different media you work in (oil paint? photography? papier mâché? sculptural string?)
- observational drawings (drawings from life) that include a variety of subject matter and both linear and volume-based work. Remember to let your own drawing style shine through.
- personal work: pieces that come from your life or experiences in a way that's meaningful to you
- your most original work. Show them your ideas and what you will bring to the art school experience.
- anything else a specific school has asked you to include, such as a sketchbook

The work in your portfolio should mostly consist of finished pieces: clean, fully realized, framed if that's relevant, and most of all, *well photographed*. The first time a school sees your work may well be in digital images. Be sure your

NATIONAL PORTFOLIO DAY

Meet with art school representatives from all over the country at National Portfolio Day.

If you can get to a city where a National Portfolio Day is being offered (and that's a *lot* of cities), it's a fantastic opportunity that should not be missed. National Portfolio Day is not one particular day—they are one-day events scheduled in many different cities where prospective art students can show their portfolios to representatives from art schools and college or university art departments. These events are free and open to the public.

What should you bring? The National Portfolio Day website says, "Your portfolio can include finished pieces, work in progress, and sketchbooks. We ask you to bring your original artwork whenever possible. We suggest that you do not spend time and money matting or framing your work. Keep your presentation simple; the work itself is what is of interest to us."

If you were a fly on the wall at National Portfolio Day, the piece of advice you would hear more than any other is "You need more observational drawing." Before you go to National Portfolio Day, be sure you have some finished observational drawings as well as your sketchbook in your portfolio.

The more well-known schools have longer lines, so take advantage of some shorter lines to talk to more art faculty and get more responses to your portfolio. Learn more about National Portfolio Day at www.nationalportfolioday.org.

photos do your work justice. Save up or get together with some friends and pool your money to hire a photographer, if you can.

THE INTERVIEW

Meeting with an art school or art department representative is an important part of the admission process. This is your opportunity to tell the school about yourself as an artist and to talk about your work and why it's important to you. It's also your chance to ask questions about the school that go a little deeper than what you can find out online.

Of course, you'll bring your portfolio and be prepared to talk about the work in it. Also be prepared to talk about

- art projects you've worked on
- why these projects were important to you
- how you've developed as an artist so far (art classes you've taken, art media you've explored, places you've visited)

"Be honest about your processes and your achievements, and don't be afraid to highlight your successes as an artist and a student. Have you contributed artwork for local galleries or events? Did you receive any honors for your work? Let the interviewers know that you are proud of your achievements and are interested in strengthening your skills. . . . Be sure you understand what the admissions committee is looking for; you might explain how you match their goals as an institution, or how you agree with the school's mission statements. Confidence in your work can go a long way."[6]—Emily Thompson

- your favorite artists and why
- why you've chosen this particular school
- what qualities you have as a person, student, and artist that would contribute to the art school experience
- what books you've read recently (beyond school assignments)

It can be hard to figure out how to present yourself at a college interview: what to wear and how to act, for example. It's important to make a good first impression, so here are some general ideas:

- Before the interview, be sure you get plenty of sleep, eat healthy food, and drink plenty of water to be at your best.
- Be reasonably well groomed. Shower, wash your hair, get the paint out from under your fingernails, brush your teeth, wear deodorant.
- Wear "business casual" clothes such as a nice dress or khakis with a button-down shirt and maybe a blazer. Save your paint-covered studio clothes for studio classes.
- Be on time. Don't do the "flaky artist" thing and show up late—that will look arrogant and like you don't care. If you don't care, they won't care.
- Shake hands like a grown-up: firm but not too firm.
- Speak up, speak clearly, answer their questions, ask your own questions, and be prepared to talk about yourself and your artwork.
- After the interview, shake hands and say thank you. As soon as you can, send an email thanking them again for the interview and expressing your interest in the school. You can also add a comment about a topic that came up during the interview.

If you can attend a National Portfolio Day event, you'll be able to practice your interviewing skills with many different schools.

Paying for Art School

Going to college these days is expensive. Art schools often have very high tuition, plus the cost of housing, food, books, expenses, and art supplies.

Art school can be expensive, so make sure your financial aid paperwork is in order.

FINANCIAL AID

It is worth your while to put some time and effort into finding out what financial aid you qualify for. Be sure to reach out to the financial aid office at the school you want to attend. They can tell you a lot about what you may be able to work out.

Financial aid can come from many sources. The kind of awards you're eligible for depends on a lot of things, things such as

- artistic merit
- academic performance in high school
- financial need

NOT ALL FINANCIAL AID IS CREATED EQUAL

Educational institutions tend to define financial aid as any scholarship, grant, loan, or paid employment that helps students pay their college expenses. Note that "financial aid" covers both *money you have to pay back* and *money you don't have to pay back*. There's a big difference!

Money You Don't Have to Pay Back

- grants
- scholarships
- work-study

Money You Have to Pay Back *with Interest*

- federal government loans
- institutional loans
- private loans

- the type of college
- your program or field

SCHOLARSHIPS

Scholarships are financial awards that are usually offered on the basis of academic or creative merit. Some scholarships are awarded for other reasons, such as membership in Scouting or some other organization, or for going into a particular field. Scholarships can also be granted to students who have certain characteristics, such as being athletes or female or a member of a minority group. Some scholarships go toward tuition; others are for something specific, like textbooks.

Merit-based art scholarships can help offset the cost of your degree, whether you attend art school or a college or university. Scholarships usually pay a portion of tuition—it is very rare to receive a full-tuition scholarship, but it does happen. Scholarships do not have to be paid back. Also, receiving a merit-based scholarship is an important credential to add to your artist résumé. Art scholarships can be local, regional, statewide, or national in scope.

You will need a portfolio to apply for art-specific scholarships. Be sure to search for art scholarships and find any and all that you might qualify for. Then follow the instructions to the letter! Don't limit yourself to art scholarships. Here are a few of the art scholarships you could start with:

- AIGA Worldstudio Scholarships
- Cynthia and Alan Baran Fine Arts and Music Scholarship Fund
- Daring Young Artists to Dream Scholarship
- Design Sponge Scholarship
- Madison Chautauqua Festival of Art Scholarship
- National YoungArts Foundation Visual Arts Scholarship
- NPG's Photo Scholarship Contest
- Scholastic Art & Writing Awards
- Young Artists Scholarship Fund

To learn more about scholarships, check out www.gocollege.com/finan cial-aid/scholarships/types/.

GRANTS

Grants are similar to scholarships. Most tuition grants are awarded based on financial need, but some are restricted to students in particular sports, academic fields, demographic groups, or with special talents. Grants do not have to be paid back.

Some grants come through federal or state agencies—for example, the Pell Grant, SMART Grants, and the Federal Supplemental Education Opportunity Grant (FSEOG). You'll need to fill out a FAFSA form (see below). Learn more about grants at https://studentaid.ed.gov/sa/types/grants-scholarships.

Grants can also come from private organizations or from the college or university itself. For instance, some private colleges or universities have enough financial resources that they can "meet 100 percent of proven financial need." That doesn't mean a free ride, but it usually means some grant money to cover the gap between what the financial aid office believes you can afford and the amount covered by scholarships and federal loans (more on federal loans below).

WORK-STUDY

The federal work-study program provides money for undergraduate and graduate students to earn money through part-time jobs. Work-study is a need-based program, so you'll need to find out if you are eligible for it. Some students are not eligible at first but become eligible later in their college career. Most jobs are on-campus, some relate to your field, but others—like working in the library—can be more general.

Some colleges and universities don't participate in the work-study program, so check with the financial aid office to see if the program's available and if you're eligible for it. It's good to apply early to have a better chance of getting the job you want most.

Since work-study is earned money (you do a job and get paid for it), this money does not need to be paid back. To learn more, check out https://student aid.ed.gov/sa/types/work-study.

FELLOWSHIPS

Fellowships are another form of earned money that can be available to students. These are short-term positions in your field. They may focus on research or professional development. Most fellowships provide a stipend that covers some of the costs associated with your education but are not enough to cover everything.

While graduate students are more frequently granted fellowships than undergraduates are, there are some schools—especially those that are committed to undergraduate research projects—that give fellowships to undergrads.

LOANS

There is always a gap between tuition and the amount of money you receive from a school in scholarships and grants. That gap is filled by student loans. Student loans have to be repaid. Interest varies, depending on the type of loan. Be sure that you understand how much interest you will be charged, when the interest starts to accumulate, and when you must start paying the loan back. Usually repayment starts when you graduate or after a six-month grace period. If you continue in school (say, going directly to grad school after getting your bachelor's degree), you can usually apply to defer payment until you're done.

Federal Loans

Federal student loans are issued by the U.S. government. They have lower interest rates and better repayment terms than other loans. You don't need anyone to cosign for your debt. If the loan is subsidized, the federal government pays the interest until you graduate. If it's unsubsidized, interest starts to accrue as soon as you accept the loan. That can amount to a very large difference in how much you pay for your education by the time the loan is paid off.

The most common federal student loan is the low-interest Stafford loan, which is available to both undergraduate and graduate students. Depending on household income, a student's Stafford loan might be subsidized or unsubsidized. (Note: Perkins loans are no longer available.)

Most schools will require you to fill out the FAFSA when you apply for financial aid. FAFSA stands for "Free Application for Federal Student Aid." Note that it doesn't say "Free Student Aid." It says "Free Application." That means it does not cost anything to apply for federal student aid. You may get "offers" to submit the FAFSA for you for a fee—this is a scam. Don't do it.

Private Loans

Chances are, federal student loans will not completely fill the gap between your tuition bill and any scholarships or grants you receive. Private student loans are issued by banks and other financial institution. Rates of interest are generally higher than for federal loans, so be careful not to borrow more than you need. Eligibility criteria for private loans are based on your (and your cosigner's) credit history.

Don't just take the first loan you find. Do some research, compare interest rates and terms. Is the interest variable or fixed? Is there a cap on the variable interest? Is the company reputable? What are their repayment requirements?

Institutional Loans

Many educational institutions make their own loans using funds provided by donors such as alumni, corporations, and foundations as well as from repayments made by prior college loan borrowers. Every college will have its own rules, terms, eligibility, and rates. Interest may be lower than private student loans, and deferment options may be better as well.

Learn more about all kinds of financial aid through the College Board website at https://bigfuture.collegeboard.org/pay-for-college.

FINANCIAL AID TIPS
- Some colleges and universities will offer tuition discounts to encourage students to attend, so tuition costs can be lower than they look at first. Competitive art schools may not offer this advantage.
- Apply for financial aid during your senior year of high school. The sooner you apply, the better your chances. Check out https://studentaid.ed.gov/sa/fafsa to see how to get started.
- Compare offers from different schools. One school may be able to match or improve on another school's financial aid offer.
- Keep your grades up. A high GPA means a lot when it comes to scholarships and grants.
- You have to reapply for financial aid every year, so you'll be filling out that FAFSA form again!
- Look for ways that loans might be deferred or forgiven. Service commitment programs are a way to use service to pay back loans.

While You're in School

Of course, while you're enrolled in college, you'll take all the courses required for your major. If you're working on a BFA degree, these will be mostly studio classes and art history, with a few other subjects to round things out. Be sure to challenge yourself to learn art forms that you've never tried before.

There are also some other important subjects you can study while you're in college that will help you as a professional artist when you graduate. Consider taking additional course work in

- marketing
- public speaking
- small business

If you haven't decided on a major yet but are still interested in art, sign up for art classes! At a smaller college, it may be difficult to get into art classes if there are a lot of majors who need those classes first. But it's always worth your while to try, so talk to the art department faculty and see what they advise.

Learn specialized art techniques by working with master art teachers.

Critiques help you see your art as others see it, learn ways to make it better, and learn how to talk about your work.

CRITIQUES

Art class critiques take some students by surprise. You hear the word "critique" and it sounds like "criticism"—like listing what's wrong with you and your work. But in an art class, critiques are an essential, objective process of analysis and evaluation of each student's work. It's not about you as a person; it's about your artwork and development as an artist.

The purpose of an art class critique is to help you learn more about how others see your work, how to work together as a supportive group, and how to offer your opinion in a useful and meaningful way.

> "Analyzing your own work will also help you develop the mindset to critique other people's work. . . . You and your classmates are in this together to be challenged and improve your art—take criticism as a tool to help you succeed and give it out as a way to help those around you succeed, too."[7]—Mary Hilliard

During a class critique, it's important to show respect to the other students as well as the teacher by following the etiquette of critiques.

When Your Work Is Being Critiqued

- Listen—don't interrupt or argue.
- Keep an open mind—even if the comments you receive seem off-base, take them in and consider them. They might turn out to be very valuable.
- Remember that what you hear is not meant as a personal attack—it's meant to be helpful.
- Restate what you hear to be sure you understand.

When You're Critiquing Others

- Be polite—remember how you feel when it's your turn.
- Keep your comments about the work, not the artist.

- Stay objective—focus on the art elements of the piece even if you don't like the style or genre.
- Avoid making value judgments (good, bad, beautiful, ugly, decorative, derivative).
- Be specific with your suggestions and keep them focused on ways to improve the piece.
- Offer helpful suggestions to everyone—don't tell your friends their work is perfect and run down everyone else's work.

INTERNSHIPS AND VOLUNTEERING

An internship is a short-term job that provides hands-on experience. An internship at a gallery or museum, or with an auction house or a professional artist, can provide experience and relationship-building opportunities like nothing else. Some internships pay a small salary, but most are unpaid; instead, you will most likely be able to earn college credit for your internship. If you don't have access to an internship, try volunteering for an arts organization.

To find an internship, you'll need to take action sooner rather than later! You may have competition for the internship you want, so the earlier you let people know you're interested, the better chance you have of being chosen.

- Talk to your advisor, the careers office, or the internship office to see if the school has a list of possible art internships or leads to find one.
- Put together a résumé showing the courses you've taken, jobs you've held, volunteer work you've done, and honors you've received.
- Contact the place where you'd like to work—gallery, museum, arts organization—and ask if they offer internships for college students and how you can apply for one.
- If the personal approach doesn't work, try an Internet search for "art internships."
- An internship might also be an opportunity to travel—where do you want to go?

But remember,

- *Do not pay a fee* to any company that claims they will find you an internship if you pay them. You shouldn't have to pay for an unpaid job.

- If you can't afford to take a part-time job or a summer job without getting paid, then taking an unpaid internship may not be a good idea.
- If you are volunteering instead of doing an internship, talk to your advisor to see if you can arrange for college credit.

BUILDING RELATIONSHIPS

As you read in chapter 2, building community and relationships are very important in the art world. Art school is a great time to get to know the other artists in your program (students and faculty) as well as the greater art community in your city. The more you interact with others, the more they will get to know you and want to work with you again. Here are some great ways to do that:

- Be a good critique participant.
- Hang out with other art students and talk about art—and everything else.
- Attend art events on and off campus.
- Work with other art students to exhibit your work.
- Be reliable and work hard.
- Travel to new places and talk to all kinds of people.
- Create opportunities for yourself and others.

"Your network is the group of like-minded, interesting, and exciting people you've invested time and energy getting to know and trust. They are the people you rely on for help and advice. Your network is your list of 'go to' people whom you trust because you've built a business or personal relationship with them. They are the people who can inspire you and open your eyes to new possibilities for your creative work and for your art business. And likewise, you offer the same support in return. Now here's the crucial ingredient that too many artists forget when it comes to networking: Helping other people is a huge part of networking!"[8]—Kesha Bruce

C. S. JENNINGS—ILLUSTRATOR

Illustrator C. S. Jennings in his Austin, Texas, studio with his illustration *The Grumpy Unicorn*.

C. S. Jennings is an illustrator from Austin, Texas. He uses graphite, Prismacolor pencils, ink, and digital media to create illustrations for many purposes. Much of his work is for children's books. He is also interested in animation, character design, and sequential storytelling. You can see more of his illustrations on his website www.csjennings.com.

What kind of art do you make?

I make commercial, publishing, and concept art. I primarily illustrate for children, with most of my work focused on books for middle grade readers. I also have done board games, video games, magazines, animation, clothing lines, and greeting cards.

How long have you been an artist?

I've done art as a job for twenty-three years.

Did you always intend to be an artist or did it happen later?

Like most kids I was obsessed with drawing. I drew with and on anything I could get my hands on. While a lot of children put away their crayons and paper for other things, I kept on drawing. "Artist" is not something I labeled myself or decided to be, it's just a part of who I am. I hoped to be able to be paid to draw, and it is nice it's worked out that way.

How did you learn your art? Did you go to college or apprentice with someone?

I took classes all throughout grade and high school. When I went to college I studied graphic design and illustration. I had a couple of teachers who were important parts in my growth as an artist. One of them remains a close friend, and yes, a mentor. I learned on the job from art directors.

How did (or didn't) your education prepare you for the different aspects of the job of artist?

Education prepared me for being an artist by helping me understand the larger art community and history in which I exist. It helped me focus in on what I really wanted to do—to draw, versus being a painter or a sculptor. It taught me how to see my own work and work with others who create as well.

It did not prepare me for the business side of art. There were no classes (then) about how to build a freelance business or where to display my work to find clients who would want to hire me.

What other jobs do you/did you do in addition to being an artist?

I've been an art director for large printing companies, a creative director for web marketing firms, and an assistant director in animation. In college I delivered pizzas for a short time until I delivered one to a T-shirt shop for whom I then became their artist.

What's the best part of being an artist?

The best part of being an artist is creating. I don't feel like myself if I don't spend some time drawing or working. Whenever I feel down, I'll sit down with my sketchbook and just draw. Sometimes I don't know what I'm going to draw, I just let my pencil move around on the paper.

What's the worst part of being an artist?

For me, the worst part (right now) of being an artist is not having enough time to create my own things. I work so much for other people, illustrating the words of their books, the concepts they have for a game, and there is not much space for my own work.

What's the most surprising thing about being an artist?

My biggest surprise is meeting people who know and love my work. My first picture book was published over a decade ago. I'll meet men and women who had my book as a kid and tell me how much a part of their childhood it was.

What advice would you give a young person who wants to be an artist?

1. Create all the time, whatever that means for you. Keep a sketchbook and pencil (or a drawing app) with you and draw in it. If you paint or sculpt, have a place where you can easily do that.

2. Draw to make you happy. Even though I do lots of work for other people, my drawings are for me. I know when a drawing is done because it brings me satisfaction. You'll have teachers who will give you grades for your art, and it's important to listen and learn from them, but find yourself and your happiness in the art you do.

3. Be kind to yourself. You don't always get the results you want on the paper or canvas—I rarely get my drawing right the first time. There is going to be someone who is a "better" artist than you. I don't think of someone as better, I think of them as different. Use other people's art to inspire you.

4. Try all of the art media. My primary drawing tool is pencil, but painting, working with clay, sitting outside working with pastels are fun vacations.

ELVIA PERRIN—PRINTMAKER

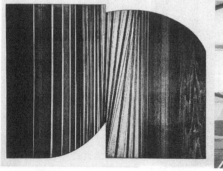

Printmaker Elvia Perrin (right) turns the wheel on the printing press; her print *Bridge* is on the left.

Elvia Perrin is a printmaker and educator. She holds a BFA from the University of Texas at Austin and an MFA from the University of North Texas. She teaches courses in design, drawing, and printmaking at Texas State University, San Marcos, and was the founding director of PrintAustin, a month-long festival celebrating contemporary art printmaking with exhibitions, demonstrations, and workshops. You can see her work on her website www.elviaperrin.com.

What kind of art do you make?
I primarily make intaglio and lithographic prints on paper.

How long have you been an artist?
I've been an artist my whole life, but professionally I would say after graduating in 2002.

When did you know you were an artist?
I knew I was artist when I was able to communicate ideas better visually.

How did you learn printmaking?
I learned about printmaking during my undergraduate work at UT Austin.

What drew you to printmaking as a medium?
Printmaking combined a lot of my loves all into one. It's very sculptural, based in material with a strong sense of drawing and making.

What are monoprints and why do you make them?
I work with intaglio and lithography processes but am drawn to monoprints—unique impressions. I use the matrix as a tool to create monoprints or individualized imagery that feels connected through image and process but can remain an individual impression.

How did (or didn't) your education prepare you for the different aspects of the job of artist?
I love education. As a student I loved learning and searching. As an educator now, I like problem solving and research, but school does not prepare you for the inconsistency of time you can put into your work. In school, your whole day revolves around learning and research about your practice. In real life, it's a balancing act between different roles we play and squeezing in time to make art.

What other jobs do you/have you done in addition to being an artist?

I teach printmaking and drawing at Texas State University in addition to being an artist.

What's the best part of being an artist?

The best thing about being an artist is the freedom to be "me," to feel happiness in creating, and to connect with material.

What's the worst part of being an artist?

The rejection and justification to others that it is a real profession is the worst part of being an artist. The money situation is very inconsistent and varies from year to year. Retirement does not seem like an option.

What's the most surprising thing about being an artist?

I have been surprisingly fortunate to connect with people who like my work. I have found a way to be my best self in making and teaching art.

Pursuing a Professional Fine Art Career

The Business of Fine Art

As a fine artist, you are creating work that expresses your vision, your beliefs, your ideas, your very soul. But you are also an entrepreneur—you are running a small business. That part of your career is more important than many artists want to realize, but you must pay attention to this fact in order to reach your ultimate goal: communicating your vision to others.

When you're a fine artist, you're also a small-business owner.

> "It's great to see artists who figure out how to cost-effectively produce and sell their artwork, and otherwise are able to combine entrepreneurship with their creative sides."[1]—Anita Campbell

ADVOCATING FOR YOUR ART

Some artists get very uncomfortable when it comes time to talk about their work and present it to others. It can seem awkward to feel that you are praising yourself or pushing yourself forward. Understand that you aren't there to talk about *yourself*. You're there to advocate for *your work*. When you keep your focus on the work itself—not on you—you'll find it much easier to talk and write about it. Remember, you are responsible for getting your work in front of the viewer. If you don't advocate for your artwork, who will?

The Boring Stuff

Who wants to do bookkeeping and taxes and databases? It's so much more fun to make art! But as an entrepreneur, you must stay organized and keep track of your artwork and your finances. Books like *Art/Work* by Heather Darcy Bhandari and Jonathan Melber and *How to Survive and Prosper as an Artist* by Caroll Michels (see Further Resources) provide excellent, detailed information on how to keep track of all the business organization that artists need to be on top of. There are also many resources for how to maintain financial records for small businesses. Remember that you're a small business! Here's the short version of what you'll need to keep track of:

- Exhibitions (Where are you showing? When? What are the dates and details? Make sure you don't promise the same piece to more than one venue at the same time.)
- Inventory (all of your artwork with medium, size, year, and price)
- Money earned (from art sales, teaching, talks, etc.)

- Money spent (on materials, rent, storage, transportation, photography, etc.)
- Paperwork (such as gallery and other contracts, consignment agreements, leases, etc.)
- Taxes (Keep your art-related and business receipts!)

Still don't want to? Here's the most important thing: The more organized you are, the easier it is to stay organized. *The more you stay organized, the more time you will have to make art.*

When you take care of your business, you're taking care of your art.

The Artist Résumé/CV

An artist's résumé has a different format from the more usual business or employment résumé. An artist's résumé is a log of what you have accomplished as an artist. It generally contains specific groupings of relevant information arranged in reverse chronological order (most recent first). See the sidebar "Résumé or CV?"

WHAT GOES IN YOUR ARTIST RÉSUMÉ?

The artist résumé is a fairly simple document, with certain expected categories in an expected order. This is not the time to introduce any fancy design ideas. Keep it clean and simple. You want whoever looks at your résumé (gallery directors, jurors, potential collectors) to be able to scan it quickly and easily. When you go to art exhibitions, check out the artist résumés for the exhibiting artists (they're usually in a binder somewhere in the gallery). You'll see different formats and categories, but they'll generally follow the format below. If you don't have anything for one of the categories, just leave that category out.

Unlike a business résumé, your artist résumé does *not* include your work history unless the work is specifically relevant to your work as an artist. If you want to apply for an art-related job (e.g., in a gallery, museum, community art organization, or art-supply store), you'll need to use a combined employment and artist résumé so that you can put your job history in as your first category.

RÉSUMÉ OR CV?

When you submit an exhibition proposal or enter certain juried shows, sometimes you'll be asked for your artist résumé and sometimes for your artist curriculum vitae (CV). What's the difference? The short answer is *length*.

Artist Résumé

An artist résumé includes the most important and most recent aspects of your art career. When you're first starting out, this may be everything. Once you've been a professional artist for a number of years, you'll want to change your headings from (for instance) "Exhibitions" to "Selected Exhibitions" and only include the best ones: most recent, most prestigious, most relevant. What you pick depends on you.

Artist CV

Your artist CV includes everything. If you are planning on teaching, you should use a standard academic CV format. If not, your CV is just the "long form" of your artist résumé. You should keep copies of both on your computer and update them at the same time. Your CV will function as a history of everything you have done and accomplished as an artist without listing individual works of art (you should keep that list separately in your inventory).

The basic format for your artist résumé or CV is as follows. See the sample résumé below for an idea of what this looks like for our pretend artist, Arty Artison.

- Contact information—at the top, either centered or right justified. Include your name, phone number, email address, website, and social media sites. Your address is optional for exhibition binders, but include it when sending portfolios or exhibition proposals to galleries.
- Biography (optional)—a short, one-paragraph history of your background, medium, style, and what you have done. You can mention places you've lived, places you've gone that have been important to you, or other art-related activities you've participated in. Longer comments should go in your statement, which is not part of your résumé.
- Education—year, degree, institution, and location in reverse chronological order (most recent first). If you have an MFA, keep your education section after your biography. If you don't have an MFA, place your education section after your exhibition history section.
- Exhibition history—exhibitions divided into solo shows followed by group shows, in reverse chronological order. Include the juror's name for juried shows.
- Collaborations/community projects—If you've done collaborative work, public art, or anything like that, include a separate section for these.
- Commissions—If you've been hired to create a work, be sure to list it here. This lets potential collectors know that you are open to creating work on commission, and it serves as a "seal of approval" by showing that other collectors think highly of your work.
- Collections—Who owns your artwork? List public collections first: institutions, businesses, and organizations. Private collections go next: individuals who own your work personally. If you want to keep your private collectors private, you can put in something like "Numerous private collections" to indicate that you have sold work to private collections.
- Awards and honors—List any awards, honors, merit scholarships, fellowships, prizes, and so forth here.
- Bibliography—List anything published about you and your work: exhibition catalogs, articles, reviews, interviews, or books, for example, that

have been published. Include the title, author, publisher or other media source, volume or issue number (if any), and date in reverse chronological order.

- Presentations—List here any artist talks you've given. If you haven't done any yet, look for an opportunity to get out there and talk about your work! An exhibition of your work is a great time to do an artist talk, but you can also do talks at schools, senior living communities, churches, Rotary or other service clubs, and Chamber of Commerce events, for example.

Some other categories you can include in your artist résumé if they're relevant are

- Teaching—If you've done some teaching but are not pursuing a college or university teaching career, list the classes you've taught along with the location and dates. If you plan to teach in a college or university, you should use an academic CV for that purpose. If you are applying for a job teaching in a community art center or the like, move this teaching section to the top, right after your education.
- Memberships—Artists groups are a great way to get to know other artists once you are out of school. There are all kinds of artists groups, from informal hangouts to collaborative collectives to critique groups. Some are focused on things you may have in common, while others are open to a wide variety of artists, which can be very helpful for learning about other perspectives.
- Publications—If you do any art writing yourself, this is where to list it. This can include journal articles, books, catalog essays, blog posts—anything that is out there for the public to read. Include the title, publisher, date, and URL (if available).

Your Artist Statement

"If I could say it in words there would be no reason to paint."[2]—Edward Hopper (attributed)

Arty Artison
123 Street Dr., Big City, Idaho 88888
208-555-5555
arty.artison@gmail.com

www.artyartisonart.com
Facebook: Arty Ariston–Artist
Instagram: @artyartisonart

ARTIST RESUME

BIO
Arty Artison is a painter who specializes in the faces and costumes of sad clowns as a reflection of her personal experience as a member of the U.S. Armed Forces serving overseas. She holds BFA and MFA degrees, and has exhibited her work nationally and internationally, as well as extensively within her home state of Idaho. Her work is held in public and private collections.

EDUCATION
2019   MFA in Painting, Yale School of Art, New Haven, CT
2016   BFA in Painting and Drawing, Idaho University–Big City

EXHIBITION HISTORY

Solo Exhibitions
2019   Arty Artison, Recent Work. Big City Art Museum, Big City, Idaho, May 21–June 30, 2019

Selected Invitational and Juried Group Exhibitions
2018   Spoils of War: Four Veterans Reflect, Big City Art Museum, Big City, Idaho, Sept. 1–30, 2018
2017   The Humor Show: Five Idaho Artists Paint Clowns, Big City Public Library, Big City, Idaho, Feb. 1–March 30, 2017
        Massive Juried Exhibition, Manhattan Art Center, Manhattan, Vermont, Jan. 1–30, 2017: Juror: Artie Smartypants, printmaker
2015   BFA Exhibition, Idaho University–Big City

Awards and Honors
2017   Best in Show, Massive Juried Exhibition, Manhattan Art Center, Manhattan, Vermont
2013   Borah Peak Art Scholarship, Idaho University Art Department

Bibliography
Spoils of War: Four Veterans Reflect catalog, September 2018
"Who Are the Artists in Your Neighborhood?" by Adele Artsville, *Manhattan Courier*, January 5, 2017

Commissions
2016   *Some Big Clown* for Jack and Donna Collectór, Peaksville, Idaho

Collections
Public Collections
  • Big City Art Museum
  • Big City Public Library
  • Manhattan Art Center
  • Big City National Bank
  • Peaksville Realty Co.
Private Collections
Numerous private collections

Presentations
2019   Artist Talk for Arty Artison, Recent Work. Big City Art Museum, Big City, Idaho, May 30, 2019
2018   Four Veterans Talk About Art for Spoils of War: Four Veterans Reflect, Big City Art Museum, Big City, Idaho, Sept. 1, 2018

This famous comment, often attributed to Edward Hopper, sums up how most artists feel about writing an artist statement. But much as we don't like writing them, and as inadequate as they feel for expressing what we do and why we do it, artist's statements are a necessary part of being an artist. In fact, Hopper himself actually had a lot to say about his work, and many of those comments would work very well in an artist's statement.

So let's look at what some other people have to say about statements.

> "Many artists assume, somewhat naively, that everyone is automatically going to 'get' or comprehend their work on the exact level on which they intend it to be perceived. Although an artist statement can be an effective tool in helping insecure people better understand your work, one does not have to be insecure about visual art to appreciate the aid of an artist statement."[3]—Caroll Michels

Fair point! Your statement is a way to help viewers find a way in to your artwork if they can't find one on their own.

> "Marketing and selling one's own artwork takes a lot of courage, and it also calls for qualities that might in other circumstances be called bad manners. You have to talk about yourself, and do a lot of it—what you do, what you have done, why you are doing it, why what you are doing has some value. . . . Most artists cannot rely on some third party to make their case. The Artist Statement is often where this case is made, but knowing what to say about oneself or one's art—and saying it in concise, grammatical, typo-free English—is rarely easy."[4]—Daniel Grant

That's another good point. Yes, it can be very uncomfortable writing about yourself in what sounds like glowing terms. But again, you aren't writing about *yourself.* You are writing about *your artwork.* Think of your artwork as a living thing that you alone are responsible for. It's your job to take care of it and help people understand it.

> "Your artist statement already exists even if you haven't written it. It's left tracks in your paintings, journals, dances, melodies. It's written all over you."[5]—Gigi Rosenberg

Well, *that's* a relief! You already know everything you need to know in order to write your statement. Here are some simple guidelines to think about.

- Write in normal English. You may have encountered "artspeak" already (especially in journals like *Art Forum*), but this kind of grandiose, pompous, yet ultimately meaningless gobbledygook is out of fashion with most artists and viewers. Don't try to show off with fancy language. Just write like you are talking to a friend or family member.

- Tell your story. Why do make your art? What materials do you use? Who or what has influenced you? Is the technique important? Does the work match a particular philosophy or school or trend or style? What do you want your audience to know?

- Read other artists' statements. You can get a very good idea of the kind of statement you do and do not want to have by reading what other artists write. Their statements will spark your own ideas of what you want to say, whether you like their statement (or their artwork) or not.

- You need long and short statements. Have a long statement that tells who you are and why you do what you do in detail. Then have a short statement of one or two paragraphs that gives the highlights. Then boil that down to one or two sentences that you can use when someone asks you what you do (this is the famous "elevator pitch").

- You should have a general statement that covers all of your work and overarching ideas. You should also have a statement about a particular series or body of work. You can even have a statement about an individual piece. You'll use all of these at different times.

- Always. Be. Writing. Like your résumé and your portfolio, your statement is not static. It's not one-and-done. You'll need to return to your statement over and over again throughout your career to update it, revise it, clarify it, or change it completely.

ART COLLECTING

Collecting art is all about forming a relationship with a work of art.

Many people collect art and for a variety of reasons. Some want to decorate their walls, some want to participate in new ideas or in history. Some are dedicated to supporting the arts or enjoy being part of the art community. Some believe that owning art enhances their social status. Some connect to a piece emotionally or spiritually. Some connect to the story behind the artwork. Some believe the art they buy will grow in financial value and make them wealthy.

For most art collectors, seeking out and finding art to own is as much a passion as making art is for the artist. Erin Thompson, in her article "Why People Collect Art," notes,

> We all know that art is a powerful way for the artist to express thoughts and feelings—but collectors know that art can serve as an expressive vehicle for collectors too. Many thus carefully curate their collections, purchasing only artworks whose display backs up a claim that the collector wishes to make.[6]

Steven Dillard answered the question "Why do you collect art?" posted on Quora by saying in part,

For me, art in a museum is like seeing animals in a zoo. I know they aren't in their natural habitat and they look sad, out of place, and I always feel so bad that I can't liberate them. . . . I think art belongs in our homes. We need to live with it. We need to love it. It's not something you visit and stare at. It's something that should be a part of your daily life. . . . Live art needs to be in the real environment, not [just] the antiseptic space of a museum.[7]

Many artists believe it's important for artists to collect art. Your collection will consist of works that speak to you and that you believe have merit. A great way to start collecting art even with little or no budget is to buy from or trade with your artist friends. Living with unique art that is different from what you make yourself will stimulate your art-making mind and bring you pleasure for the rest of your life.

Promoting Your Artwork

Artists can be uncomfortable with terms like "promoting" or "marketing," but your job as a professional fine artist, as an art entrepreneur, and as your art's advocate is letting people get to know your artwork.

PHOTOGRAPHING YOUR WORK

It is very important to have excellent photographs of your artwork that show each piece to its best advantage. If you're a photographer, you can learn how to take photos of your work yourself. But it's a tricky process to get the light just right, and it's different for 2-D versus 3-D artwork. Many artists find it's better to hire a photographer who has a specific expertise in photographing artwork. Prices vary, so you'll need to do your homework to find an affordable art photographer in your area. The best way is to talk with other artists as well as local galleries and museums to discover which photographers they recommend.

You'll need to have both high- and low-resolution images.

- High-resolution (300 dpi) images should be between 5,000 and 10,000 kB. TIFF files have the most information, so you should have them; but you will usually submit JPG files. JPG files are compressed and lose a little information when saved; TIFF files are not compressed. High-res images are used for print (such as exhibition announcements, magazines, posters, etc.). Some juried exhibitions want high-res files as well.

- Low-resolution (72 dpi) files are used online for your website and social media and to email to prospective galleries and collectors. Low-res files are smaller, so they upload and download much more quickly than high-res files. Use an image program like Adobe Photoshop or something similar to save copies of your high-res JPG files as low-res JPG files.

The photos themselves *must* be

- in focus
- true to the color of the original artwork
- free of hotspots and shadows
- cropped to the edges (no background showing) for 2-D work
- against a plain background for 3-D work

YOUR ONLINE PRESENCE

The Internet is an important tool for advocating for your work. Your website is your online portfolio. Your Instagram, Twitter, and other social media accounts are where you tell your story. Your mailing list is how you keep your best followers up to date on what you're doing and what's coming up for your artwork.

Your Website

Every artist needs a website. Your website is your online portfolio. It's the place to showcase your work in an organized way for the world to see. Shop around for the website platform that meets your needs best. For instance, free sites are available but may require you to include their name in your URL. If you want to sell work directly from your site, you may want to get a site with an e-commerce option, and you'll want to list prices for your pieces. If you want your website to be a "pure" portfolio (e.g., if you are represented by a commercial gallery), then you don't want to list your prices.

In general, your website should contain

- a home page with links to the other pages.

- an About page with your bio and statement and a link to. . . .
- your résumé or CV. This can be complete or it can be a "selected" list with only your most impressive credentials.
- a contact page with a form visitors can use to get in touch with you. Be sure to use a CAPTCHA to keep out the bots (but be aware that even with a CAPTCHA, you will be contacted by scammers through your contact page from time to time).
- portfolio pages for each series you want to show. These should have small images for each artwork you are showing in the series that link to. . . .
- individual artwork pages, one for each piece. These pages should have a larger 72 dpi image of one piece with the usual information (medium, size, and price if you're listing prices).
- if you are listing prices, it is also good to have a single page that is your price list for all the pieces on the website.
- a link to sign up for your e-newsletter (see "Your Mailing List" below).

Keep the design of your site clear and simple. Think about it from the visitor's point of view and make it easy to navigate. Avoid things that move and jump around, and anything noisy (including music) that starts immediately on its own. If video is part of your work or necessary to understand your work, set it to start when the visitor clicks on it.

Your Social Media

Social media accounts are the place to show your latest work, show your works in progress, announce your news, and follow other artists and influencers. Most artists currently like Instagram because it's all about images. But Twitter also accepts images, and if you can keep your comments short, Twitter can be a useful way to share your work as well. Some artists have Facebook pages, but Instagram and Twitter will reach a much wider audience.

Social media changes too quickly for any tips given here to stay relevant. You'll want to keep informed about those changes and stay up to date on any expert recommendations for artists using social media. However, following are some general points.

- Post images frequently.
- Post high-quality images. These can include finished work, work in progress, videos of you in the studio, photos or videos of exhibitions you're in, and artwork in museums that you like with your comments, for example.
- Only post selfies if they are relevant to your life and work as an artist.
- Use relevant hashtags.
- Follow other artists as well as galleries, museums, art consultants, interior designers, and architects as well as the people you already know.
- Comment on other people's posts.
- Don't pay for followers. There are people who will offer to connect you to thousands of followers, but those won't be real followers. They won't be following you because they're interested in your work.

Your Mailing List

Your mailing list consists of people who have expressed an interest in your work or who might be interested in your work. Your list should include names, mailing addresses, and email addresses. If you can include phone numbers and notes on who the person is and why they're on the list, so much the better. Possible categories are

- friends and family
- people in your local art community
- people who have signed up to be on your mailing list
- anyone who ever handed you a business card
- movers and shakers in your community
- members of museum or nonprofit arts organization boards
- other artists in the community

You can keep the list yourself in a spreadsheet program like Excel or Google Sheets or you can keep it online on an email marketing site like Mailchimp or ConstantContact. If you use a site like Mailchimp or ConstantContact, you can send an email newsletter to your mailing list monthly, quarterly, or whenever you have news. Mailchimp has a free plan and allows as many images as you're likely to need to upload.

You might also want to keep a "postcard list" with the names and addresses of people you'd like to invite to art exhibitions but don't want to include on your email list, for whatever reason.

Keep track of your mailing list and make sure it's as current as you can make it. This will take time, but it's worth it. The people who sign up for your

> "Most of us know the feeling of being moved by a work of art, whether it is a song, a play, a poem, a novel, a painting, or a spatio-temporal experiment. When we are touched, we are moved; we are transported to a new place that is, nevertheless, strongly rooted in a physical experience, in our bodies. We become aware of a feeling that may not be unfamiliar to us but which we did not actively focus on before. This transformative experience is what art is constantly seeking."[8]—Olafur Eliasson

mailing list through your website are your best followers. They have chosen to be there!

Talking about Your Artwork

Talking about your work in person is one of the best ways there is to help viewers understand what your goals with your artwork are. There are many opportunities to talk about your artwork—wherever you go, when people learn you are an artist, they will want to ask you about your work. Be prepared to answer them!

TALKING TO PEOPLE AT AN ART SHOW OR OPENING

When you show work in an art exhibition, people will be looking at it, wondering about it, and wanting to ask you questions. Be sure that you are available, wear a name tag so that visitors know which person in the room is the artist,

Look for opportunities to talk to people about your art and why you make it.

and be friendly. Here are some quick tips for talking to people about your work in an informal setting, like a conversation:

1. There are no stupid questions. People will ask you questions about aspects of your piece that seem obvious to you. Understand that they don't see things the same way you do. Assume the question is sincere and not snarky. Answer it!

2. Your point of view is not the only valid one. Viewers bring themselves to artwork, and what they see in it may be very different from what you meant. That's okay! In fact, that's good. It means your piece has a life beyond your original idea. Let them tell you their ideas. You might learn something about the piece you didn't recognize before. If you don't agree, be polite and respond with something like "That's an interesting perspective."

3. If someone is spending time with your piece but doesn't ask you a question, go ahead and ask them one. Ask them what they're noticing or to tell you their response. Then be silent, so they have room to respond.

GIVING A FORMAL ARTIST TALK

Look for opportunities to talk about your work. This can be during an opening of an exhibition your artwork is in or at a special event set up in connection with a show. You can also speak at schools, senior centers, Rotary or Chamber of Commerce events, libraries, service organizations, business and professional groups, "brown bag" lunch groups, adult education settings, or anywhere else that brings in speakers or where small or large groups can gather. You can bring some artwork to talk about or you can give a slide show if you can't bring actual work. Some organizations even pay a small speaker's fee for artist talks.

Some artists find giving a talk easy and natural. Others are intimidated by the idea of speaking in public. Here are some tips to make it easier:

- Remind yourself that you are the expert on your own work.
- Remember that the audience is there because they are interested in and curious about what you do, how you do it, and why you do it.
- Be prepared—plan what you are going to say and how long it will take.
- Have good images—if you're doing a slide show, be sure to review your images ahead of time so that you can see if they look washed out or faded.
- Introduce yourself and say what you do and what you're going to talk about.
- Remember to smile and make eye contact with different members of the audience.
- Talk to somebody—pick one person in the audience and talk to them. Then switch to another individual, and then another.
- Leave time for questions and answer them in a simple and straightforward manner.
- Don't rush out—people from the audience may want to speak to you individually after the talk. Take this chance to build relationships.

Beyond Business

While you are advocating for your art and building your art business, remember why you're doing this. Artists don't usually make art in order to make lots of money. In fact, artists often don't make much money at all. But if you can

The business of art is important, but the most important thing is the joy and passion of creating.

"Most folks block out emotion. Then, suddenly, a painting 'speaks' to them. At that point, the artist has done their job. For me, it is wonderful to connect with people through my work—when people respond to a painting and really 'feel'"[9]—Lesley Birch

sustain your creative practice financially, you will be able to sustain it in every other way that counts. That includes time you spend making art, time you spend collaborating with others on art and art-related projects, time you spend enjoying the company of other artists, and the time you spend letting your mind wander wherever it wants to go to feed your soul and your work.

As a professional fine artist, you get to make artwork and make art work. You get to interact with the art world, hang with other artists (visual artists, performing artists, writers, actors, musicians, and all the other creative types out there). You will meet people who love your work, people who want and collect your work, and people who can't stand your work. You will face rejection over and over again, which will make each acceptance that much sweeter.

Sometimes you will have trouble staying motivated, thinking of where to go or what to do next, or why to continue to make art when you could have gone to law school. That's all part of the job. By living the life of a professional fine artist, you will discover that creativity ebbs and flows like the tide, that not everyone likes or appreciates what you make and that's okay, and that there are always ideas for you as long as you stay open to them. You will learn the value of what you do and how to be the best advocate you can be for your artwork in the world. You may be discouraged sometimes, but you will never be bored.

Cookie Washington, fiber artist, quilter, and independent curator. Left: *Goddess of Transition.* Right: *Eternal Feminine.*

COOKIE WASHINGTON—FIBER ARTIST

Torreah "Cookie" Washington is a well-known fiber artist/quilter and exhibition curator from the Charleston, South Carolina, area. She works primarily on commission and focuses on Afrocentric themes. For more than a decade, she has curated an annual juried exhibition featuring the work of African American fiber artists in North Charleston.

What kind of art do you make?

I call myself a fiber artist or an art quilter. I find that textile design emits a spirit, a presence, an energy, a vitality unlike that of any other medium. I use machine and hand sewing, painting, surface design, embellishment, found objects, photography, and other nontraditional materials. Merging commonly accepted fabric with uncommon materials creates more of an appliquéd pictorial tapestry. Blending these elements allows me to express visually what cannot be spoken. The narrative themes in my murals are color intense, making statements that can be either humorous or serious. I am concerned as much with art as with craft. I draw inspiration from ancient cultures, modern art from Africa, and the art of the Americas.

How long have you been an artist?

I have been creating with textiles for more than three decades. My current passion is fiber art muralism that celebrates the Divine Feminine and the contributions of her African ancestral heritage. I have been a fiber artist of some sort my whole life.

Did you always intend to be an artist or did it happen later?

I have been a fiber artist of some sort my whole life. When I was four years old, my Granddaddy paid me fifty cents for the first "Barbie" dress I ever designed. I was sewing all my own clothes by the age of thirteen. Throughout high school in New Mexico and university in Maryland, I continued to sew, knit, and pursue many other crafts.

How did you learn your art?

I'm a fourth-generation textile artist. My mother, grandmother, and great-grandmother were all experienced quilters, fashion designers, and master tailors. I am a mostly self-taught quilt artist. I have learned from books, studying other artists, and a few quilting classes. I like to create works that blur the lines between quilts, wall hangings, wearable art, soft sculpture, and installation.

What other jobs do you/did you do in addition to being an artist?

I originally studied nursing, but after I married and my children were born, I felt it was vitally important to stay home with them, so I started my dressmaking business in earnest. Fashion design and dressmaking is a serious art form. I loved the ability to take flat fabric and sculpt it into a wedding dress, a jacket, a handbag, whatever. I created the Kissbag (1999), a pyramid-shaped evening bag that has been described as "the shape of things to come, a bag for a new millennium." My specialty bags are now being carried by such Hollywood luminaries as Camryn Manheim, Cher, Star Jones, and Dame Judi Dench.

How did you begin curating?

I live in Charleston, South Carolina, which has been described as Ellis Island for people who came here as slaves. Between 40 and 60 percent of everyone who came to the Americas as a slave came through Charleston. But there was no African American gallery there. The city of North Charleston has been very supportive of African American artists and individual artists, and they have been very good to me. I thought quilting should be an arm of the North Charleston arts festival—now we're in our thirteenth year. We have African American artists from all over the country. They're an amazingly diverse group and so talented. I'm so honored to put this show together every year and meet these artists, mostly women. I think that I'm informing the public and showing them a different side of art and art history.

What's the best part of being an artist?

Telling stories. Making people aware of things. I want to make art that challenges people to think and feel, art that uplifts and annoys, art that challenges them to learn more about the subject and their own feelings about it. I have a fire in the belly, a passionate urge to create art that is griot in nature—more teaching and healing than divisive. I want the viewer to come away changed for the better after having experienced my work. I want my art to make you feel informed; I am not at all interested in creating art that matches your furniture.

What's the worst part of being an artist?

Not getting paid and not getting taken seriously. I think people think that art comes about by magic—like the story of the shoemaker and the elves. They don't understand the work that goes into it. I don't do quilts that are going to be like anyone else's, and they take a long time and hard work.

What's the most surprising thing about being an artist?

It's like my vocation, my ministry. It feeds my soul. That is surprising. In the midst of all the craziness in the world, art is my port in a storm, my candle on the water. It is a blessing.

What advice would you give a young person who wants to be an artist?

Notes

Introduction

1. Aleta Michaletos, "What Is the Artist's Role in Society?" www.artworkarchive .com/blog/what-is-the-artist-s-role-in-society.

2. Jasper Johns, quoted in "The Story behind Jasper Johns's Iconic and Experimental Crosshatched Works," Sotheby's, October 17, 2018, www.sothebys.com/en /articles/the-story-behind-jasper-johnss-iconic-and-experimental-crosshatched-works.

3. Constance Smith, *Art Marketing 101: A Handbook for the Fine Artist* (Nevada City, CA: ArtNetwork, 2000), 19.

Chapter 1

1. David Bayles and Ted Orland, *Art & Fear: Observations on the Perils (and Rewards) of Artmaking* (Santa Barbara, CA: Capra Press, 1993), 117.

2. Georgia O'Keeffe, letter to Sherwood Anderson, 1924.

3. Jasper Johns, quoted in "Take an Object: August 22, 2015–February 28, 2016," Museum of Modern Art, www.moma.org/calendar/exhibitions/1549.

4. Kathie Sorensen and Steve Crabtree, "Exactly What Is Talent, Anyway? Knowledge and Skills Can Be Learned, But Talent Is Enduring," *Gallup Business Journal*, October 2, 2000, https://news.gallup.com/businessjournal/412/exactly-what-tal ent-anyway.aspx.

5. Paul Dorrell, "Excerpts from Paul's Book, *Living the Artist's Life*," July 23, 2018, www.leopoldgallery.com/excerpts-from-pauls-book-living-the-artists-life/.

6. Michelangelo, www.michelangelo.org/michelangelo-quotes.jsp.

7. Vincent Van Gogh, letter to Theo Van Gogh, September 24, 1880.

8. Vincent Van Gogh, letter to Theo Van Gogh from Drenthe, October 28, 1883.

9. Tate, "Art Term: Installation Art," www.tate.org.uk/art/art-terms/i/installa tion-art.

10. Metropolitan Museum of Art, "What Is Printmaking?" www.metmuseum .org/about-the-met/curatorial-departments/drawings-and-prints/materials-and-tech niques/printmaking.

11. Lee Hammon, "Why We Make Art," ArtistsNetwork, www.artistsnetwork
.com/art-inspiration/why-we-make-art-lee-hammond/.

12. Clay Wirestone, "11 Celebrated Artists Who Didn't Quit Their Day Jobs,"
Mentalfloss, August 11, 2018, http://mentalfloss.com/article/52293/11-celebrated-art
ists-who-didnt-quit-their-day-jobs.

Chapter 2

1. Jasper Johns, quoted in "Daily Close-up, after the Flag" by Roberta Brandes
Gratz, *New York Post*, December 30, 1970, 25.

2. Ginny Sykes, quoted in "What Is the Artist's Role in Society?" Artwork
Archive, www.artworkarchive.com/blog/what-is-the-artist-s-role-in-society.

3. Caroll Michels, *How to Survive and Prosper as an Artist: Selling Yourself without
Selling Your Soul*, 5th ed. (New York: Henry Holt, 2001), 156.

4. Gigi Rosenberg, *The Artist's Guide to Grant Writing: How to Find Funds and
Write Foolproof Proposals for the Visual, Literary, and Performing Artist* (New York: Watson-Guptill, 2010), 2.

5. Jason Horejs, "Hosting a Successful Open Studio," RedDotBlog, September
22, 2015, https://reddotblog.com/hosting-a-successful-open-studio/.

6. Heather Darcy Bhandari and Jonathan Melber, *Art/Work: Everything You Need
to Know (and Do) As You Pursue Your Art Career* (New York: Free Press, 2017), 275.

7. Andrew Gordon, "How to Get a Job at Pixar," Creative Bloq, October 25,
2012, www.creativebloq.com/animation/job-at-pixar-10121018.

Chapter 3

1. Mary Hilliard, "10 Things You Should Know before Attending Art School,"
Her Campus, March 17, 2018, www.hercampus.com/high-school/10-things-you-
should-know-attending-art-school.

2. Nigel Carrington, quoted in "Why Is It Still a Good Idea for Young Creatives to Go to Art School?" by Rob Alderson, It's Nice That, October 6, 2014, www
.itsnicethat.com/articles/why-go-to-art-school.

3. Christina Macres, "How to Get into Art School," ArtBistro, May 17, 2010,
http://artbistro.monster.com/education/articles/10997-how-to-get-into-art-school.

4. Hilliard, "10 Things You Should Know."

5. "Regional vs. National Accreditation—There's a Huge Difference," EDsmart website, July 10, 2019,https://www.edsmart.org/regional-vs-national-accreditation/.

6. Emily Thompson, "5 Things You Must Do When Applying to Art College," CreativeBloq, July 28, 2018, www.creativebloq.com/career/how-get-art-college-5132555.

7. Hilliard, "10 Things You Should Know."

8. Kesha Bruce, "Networking for Artists Part #2, Making Connections: How to Start Conversations That Matter," FineArtViews, May 29, 2013, https://fineartviews.com/blog/60641/networking-for-artists-part-2-making-connections-how-to-start-conversations-that-matter.

Chapter 4

1. Anita Campbell, "The Trend of the Artist Entrepreneur," Small Business Trends, November 1, 2017, https://smallbiztrends.com/2008/11/the-trend-of-the-artist-entrepreneur.html.

2. This quote has been widely attributed to Edward Hopper but is not included in sources that quote his actual words. To read what Hopper really said about his work and art in general, visit https://en.wikiquote.org/wiki/Edward_Hopper.

3. Caroll Michels, *How to Survive and Prosper as an Artist: Selling Yourself without Selling Your Soul*, 5th ed. (New York: Henry Holt, 2001), 51.

4. Daniel Grant, *Selling Art without Galleries: Toward Making a Living from Your Art* (New York: Allworth Press, 2006), 191.

5. Gigi Rosenberg, *The Artist's Guide to Grant Writing: How to Find Funds and Write Foolproof Proposals for the Visual, Literary, and Performing Artist* (New York: Watson-Guptill, 2010), 89.

6. Erin Thompson, "Why People Collect Art," Aeon, August 23, 2016, https://aeon.co/essays/what-drives-art-collectors-to-buy-and-display-their-finds.

7. Steven Dillard responding to the question "Why do you collect art?" Quora, April 11, 2013, www.quora.com/Why-do-you-collect-art.

8. Olafur Eliasson, "Why Art Has the Power to Change the World," World Economic Forum, January 18, 2016, www.weforum.org/agenda/2016/01/why-art-has-the-power-to-change-the-world/.

9. Lesley Birch, quoted in "What Is the Artist's Role in Society?" Artwork Archive, www.artworkarchive.com/blog/what-is-the-artist-s-role-in-society.

Glossary

3-D (three-dimensional) art: Artwork that has volume such as sculpture, ceramics, reliefs, and installations.

2-D (two-dimensional) art: Artwork that is essentially flat such as paintings on canvas and works on paper.

academic CV: A curriculum vitae that is used to apply for teaching jobs at the college and university level.

anatomy: The study of the human figure, including bones, musculature, surface structures, proportion, and movement.

art collaborative: Several artists who work together on artwork that is distinct from the work each artist does on his or her own.

art critic: A person who evaluates works or bodies of art and presents an opinion in a public forum such as a newspaper, art journal, or web page.

art fair/art festival: Periodic events, often held outdoors in parks or other public spaces, where artists and craftspeople can sell their work directly to visitors.

art fair, major: Annual or biannual events in which galleries pay to participate and set up a "mini-gallery" to present the work of their artists.

art market: The buying and selling of art, including those who buy and sell. The term "primary art market" refers to the first time an artwork is sold, while "secondary art market" refers to any time artworks are resold. Artists usually only receive payment from the primary art market.

art therapy: A type of psychotherapy that uses art-making and creativity for therapeutic purposes.

art world: Everyone who participates in the making, showing, selling, commissioning, buying, promoting, preserving, or critiquing of fine art.

artist: A person who makes art.

artist collective: A group of artists who work together toward shared aims.

artist groups: Artists who get together periodically for networking, conversation, support, and critiques.

artist's CV: A complete description of an artist's career in list form.

artist's résumé: A short and selective list of the highlights of an artist's career.

artist's statement: A written account of an artist's purpose and intent in his or her overall work or in a specific body of work.

arts district: A neighborhood that has been formally or informally designated the arts center of a particular city or town.

BFA: A bachelor of fine arts degree.

body of work: All of the pieces ever made by a single artist (sometimes called the artist's "oeuvre").

collection: A group of artworks owned by an individual, museum, corporation, or any other institution.

collector: A person who purchases artwork.

commercial gallery: A business that sells the artwork of a chosen group of artists either on consignment or by contract.

commission on sales: The percentage of the sales price of an artwork that is retained by the gallery or art dealer who sells it.

commission, working on: Creating a specific work of art for a client or patron.

commodity: A thing that can be bought, sold, or owned.

creative: To have the ability to make something that did not previously exist; used in the business world to refer to a person who does creative work such as a graphic artist or copywriter.

criticism: The discussion or evaluation of a work of art, usually in terms of its perceived quality.

critique: The process of describing and analyzing a work of art. In the classroom, critiques are a regular part of the learning process in which the teacher and other students give their responses to a particular piece and discuss its qualities, both positive and negative. It is a useful process for both those giving and those receiving the critique.

curated exhibition: An art exhibition in which certain works have been selected by one individual (the curator) for aesthetic, historical, or social reasons.

curator, exhibition: A person who curates an exhibition by choosing which artworks will be included. Some artists curate exhibitions independently (not as employees of galleries or museums).

curator, museum: A person employed by a museum or other institution to manage a collection of art or other artifacts.

digital images: A computer file consisting of picture elements called "pixels." High-resolution digital images usually have at least 300 pixels per square inch at full size and are used for printed images. Low-resolution digital images usually have 72 pixels per square inch and are used online. Common digital image types are JPG, PNG, TIFF, GIF, and Post-Script.

e-newsletter: Also called an "email newsletter," this is a communication sent out to a group of subscribers on a regular or semiregular basis as part of a marketing campaign.

entrepreneur: A person who starts, organizes, and manages a business and is responsible for the financial risk involved.

exhibition: Presentation of a group of artworks or artifacts to the public; exhibitions can be temporary or permanent.

fine art: Artwork (especially visual art) that exists for its aesthetic, intellectual, or imaginative content.

gallery: A room or building where artwork is displayed. See also **commercial gallery** and **nonprofit gallery**.

grant: A sum of money given to an individual artist or to a venue for the purpose of supporting, developing, or exhibiting art.

instagram: A social-media platform for sharing images.

juried exhibition: A short-term art show where artwork is chosen by a juror (or jurors) from among a group of submitted images. Juried shows typically charge artists a fee to submit images and issue a prospectus defining what kind of artwork is being sought.

linear: Artwork that emphasizes line over other qualities.

marginalized: People, groups, or ideas that are treated as insignificant by society.

market: See **art market**.

marketing: Promoting and selling a product to appropriate clientele, including the research, communication, advertising, and exchange involved in promoting and selling the product.

MFA: A master of fine arts degree.

media/medium: The techniques and tools used to create an artwork.

museum: An institution (either public or private) that exists to collect, curate, care for, promote the study of, and display objects of cultural or scientific importance or value, such as art.

networking: Building and cultivating relationships in a particular field or business.

nonprofit gallery: An organization or institution that exhibits art without the intention of selling it for profit. These can include community art centers, artists' cooperatives, artist-run spaces, college and university galleries, and museums.

observational drawing: Drawing from direct observation of real objects, animals, and people.

online portfolio: Organized presentation of an artist's work in digital images on a website or social media site.

open studio: A combination social and exhibition event in which artists welcome visitors into their workspace to see their art and how they make it, with the ultimate goal of selling work and developing relationships with collectors.

outsider artist: A self-taught artist who has little or no contact with the art world or art institutions, including artists with mental illness or from traditional communities.

patron: A person who supports the arts, often by purchasing artwork, providing a regular stipend to an artist, or making financial contributions to arts institutions.

percent-for-art: State-run programs that designate a certain percentage of the budget for a state-funded building project will be used for the purchase or commissioning of artwork.

portfolio: Artworks selected by an artist to share with potential galleries or collectors that best represent the artist's style and current work.

poseur: Someone who pretends to be something they are not, especially in an affected and insincere way; someone who "puts on airs."

proposal: A document submitted by an artist for consideration for an exhibition or a grant consisting of a description of the project, the rationale for funding the project, a budget, images that help define the project, and other material in support of the project.

public art: Commissioned art that is intended for permanent display in a public space.

relief: Sculpture that combines 2-D and 3-D elements and projects from a wall or other flat surface. "Low-relief" includes everything from incised lines to shallow sculpture. "High-relief" refers to figures or elements closest to complete 3-D.

series: A group of works by an artist that have common characteristics such as visual elements, ideas, themes, materials, or techniques.

small business: An independently owned and operated business with fewer than five hundred employees. Artists who sell their artwork are sole proprietors of a small business, whether they are incorporated as one or not.

talent: A natural aptitude for something (such as making art).

venue: The place where an event, such as an art exhibition, takes place (e.g., a gallery, museum, or park).

viewer: A person (real or potential).

visual art: Art that is created to be seen, which can include 2- and 3-D fine art forms as well as decorative art. Many art disciplines (film, video, performance, theater) also include aspects of visual art.

volumetric: 2-D artwork that conveys a sense of volume or three-dimensionality such as a drawing with more emphasis on light and shadow than on line.

wall-hung art: 2-D and 3-D art that is intended to be hung on a wall such as a painting, drawing, art print, relief sculpture, or photograph. Wall-hung art is frequently framed, although there are many exceptions.

Further Resources

Books to Buy and Keep for a Lifetime

These books are among the best overviews of what it means to be a fine artist (yes, even the one with "writing" in the title). Buy them, read them, make notes in the margins, and (most importantly) reread them at different times throughout your life.

Bayles, David, and Ted Orland. *Art & Fear: Observations on the Perils (and Rewards) of Artmaking*. Santa Barbara, CA: Capra Press, 1993.

> *Art & Fear* explores the way art gets made, the reasons it often doesn't get made, and the nature of the difficulties that cause so many artists to give up along the way. The book's coauthors, David Bayles and Ted Orland, are themselves both working artists, grappling daily with the problems of making art in the real world. Their insights and observations, drawn from personal experience, provide an incisive view into the world of art as it is experienced by artmakers themselves. "Today, more than it was however many years ago, art is hard because you have to keep after it so consistently. On so many different fronts. For so little external reward. Artists become veteran artists only by making peace not just with themselves, but with a huge range of issues. You have to find your work."

Cameron, Julia. *The Artist's Way: A Spiritual Path to Higher Creativity*. New York: Jeremy P. Tarcher, 2002.

> *The Artist's Way* is the seminal book on the subject of creativity. An international bestseller, millions of readers have found it to be an invaluable guide to living the artist's life. Still as vital today—or perhaps even more so—than it was when it was first published almost two decades ago, it is a powerfully provocative and inspiring work.

King, Stephen. *On Writing: A Memoir of the Craft*. New York: Pocket Books, 2000.

> Stephen King's memoir is a classic not only for writers (his intended audience) but for anyone pursuing a creative practice. "This is not an autobiography. It is, rather, a kind of *curriculum vitae*—my attempt to show how one writer was formed. Not how one writer was *made*; I don't believe writers *can* be made, either by circumstances or by self-will (although I did believe those things once). . . . I believe large numbers of people have at least some talent as writers and storytellers, and that those talents can be strengthened and sharpened. If I didn't believe that, writing a book like this would be a waste of time."

Loudon, Sharon, ed. *Living and Sustaining an Artist's Life: Essays by 40 Working Artists*. Bristol, UK: Intellect Books, 2013.

> In this day and age, as art has become more and more of a commodity, many students graduating from art school believe that they will immediately make a living as an artist by obtaining gallery representation. One of the goals of this book is to dispel the belief that there is only one way to chart a path into a creative and sustainable life as an artist. This collection of essays is intended to show the reality of how artists—from the unknown to the established—juggle their creative lives with the everyday needs of making a living. They share with us in their own words how they are creative inside and outside the studio, both on a day-to-day basis and over the long haul.

Resources about Fine Arts

These online resources address common questions about what it's like to be a fine artist, what types of art media exist, and where being an artist can take you.

Dodge, Krystle. *What Jobs Can I Get with a Bachelor of Fine Arts Degree?* Degree query. www.degreequery.com/jobs-can-get-bachelor-fine-arts-degree/.

Garner, Christine. "Traditional Art Mediums." Medium. September 7, 2018. https://medium.com/the-art-squirrel/traditional-art-mediums-4d38f 4da88ce.

Princeton Review. "A Day in the Life of a Digital Artist." www.princetonreview
.com/careers/201/digital-artist.

Quacquarelli Symonds. "What Can You Do with an Art Degree?" www
.topuniversities.com/student-info/careers-advice/what-can-you-do-art-de
gree.

Southeastern Louisiana University. "What Can I Do with My Visual Arts
Degree?" www.southeastern.edu/acad_research/programs/cse/career_expl
/slu_degree/degrees/visual_arts.html.

Study.com. "Visual Artist Career: Job Description & Career Requirements."
https://study.com/articles/Visual_Artist_Job_Description_and_Require
ments_for_a_Career_in_the_Visual_Arts.html.

Tate. "Art Terms." www.tate.org.uk/art/art-terms.

visual-arts-cork.com. "Types of Art." www.visual-arts-cork.com/art-types
.htm#types.

Resources about Art School

These online resources provide a wealth of information about applying for art
school.

Gale, Amiria. "How to Make an Art Portfolio for College or University (The
Ultimate Guide)." Student Art Guide. October 19, 2018. www.student
artguide.com/articles/how-to-make-an-art-portfolio-for-college-or-uni
versity.

"Lauren." "Tips for Preparing Your Art School Portfolio." Peterson's. www
.petersons.com/blog/tips-for-preparing-your-art-school-portfolio/.

Macres, Christina. "How to Get into Art School." ArtBistro. May 17, 2010.
http://artbistro.monster.com/education/articles/10997-how-to-get-into-
art-school.

Niche.com. "2019 Best Colleges for Art in America." www.niche.com/colleges
/search/best-colleges-for-art/.

NPDA (National Portfolio Day). Home page. https://nationalportfolioday
.org/.

———. "Members." https://nationalportfolioday.org/members/.

———. "Past Events." https://nationalportfolioday.org/past-events/.

Pelissier, Sandrine. "Work of Art: 12 Tips on How to Create a Perfect Art Portfolio." Bluprint. March 21, 2014. https://shop.mybluprint.com/art/article/how-to-create-an-art-portfolio/.

Rhode Island School of Design. "First-Year Admissions: Apply to RISD." www.risd.edu/admissions/first-year/apply/.

———. "Transfer Admissions: Apply to RISD." www.risd.edu/admissions/transfer/apply/.

Thompson, Emily. "5 Things You Must Do When Applying to Art College." Creative Bloq. July 28, 2018. www.creativebloq.com/career/how-get-art-college-5132555.

Zdunek, Jessica. "Tips on Compiling a Portfolio for Art Scholarships." *U.S. News & World Report.* July 7, 2016. www.usnews.com/education/scholarship-search-insider/articles/2016-07-07/tips-on-compiling-a-portfolio-for-art-scholarships.

Resources about Art Careers

These online and print resources cover different aspects of having a successful art career.

WORKING AS AN ARTIST

Artwork Archive. "What Does It Take to Make It as an Artist?" www.artworkarchive.com/blog/what-does-it-take-to-make-it-as-an-artist.

Association of Medical Illustrators. Home page. www.ami.org.

The Balance Careers. "Job Profiles." www.thebalancecareers.com/arts-career-profiles-4161776.

Bamberger, Alan. "Making Art on Commission: Tips for Artists." ArtBusiness.com. www.artbusiness.com/privcom.html.

Bhandari, Heather Darcy, and Jonathan Melber. *Art/Work: Everything You Need to Know (and Do) As You Pursue Your Art Career.* New York: Free Press, 2017.

ExploreHealthCareers.org. "Medical Illustrator/Animator." https://explorehealthcareers.org/career/arts-and-humanities-in-health/medical-illustrator-animator/.

Hammond, Lee. "Why We Make Art." ArtistsNetwork. www.artistsnetwork
.com/art-inspiration/why-we-make-art-lee-hammond/.

Lawrence, Hannah. "5 Myths about Being an Artist: Debunked." Acceptd.
April 30, 2018. https://getacceptd.com/5-myths-about-being-an-artist-de
bunked/.

Nixon, Andrew. "Meet the Artist: Sandra Porter RWA." The Floating Circle.
January 13, 2019. https://floatingcircle-rwa.org/2019/01/13/meet-the-
artist-sandra-porter-rwa-ma/.

THE BUSINESS OF ART

Grant, Daniel. *Selling Art without Galleries: Toward Making a Living from Your
Art.* New York: Allworth Press, 2006.

Larsson, Naomi. "How to Make a Living from Your Art: Young Artists Share
Their Stories." *Guardian.* www.theguardian.com/education/2018/oct/30
/how-to-make-a-living-from-your-art-young-artists-share-their-stories.

Michels, Caroll. *How to Survive and Prosper as an Artist: Selling Yourself without
Selling Your Soul,* 5th ed. New York: Henry Holt, 2001.

Rosenberg, Gigi. *The Artist's Guide to Grant Writing: How to Find Funds and
Write Foolproof Proposals for the Visual, Literary, and Performing Artist.* New
York: Random House, 2010.

Stanfield, Alyson B. *I'd Rather Be in the Studio: The Artist's No-Excuse Guide to
Self-Promotion.* Golden, CO: Pentas Press, 2011.

PRESENTING YOUR ART WORK

Blakeslee, Carolyn, ed. *Getting Exposure: The Artist's Guide to Exhibiting the
Work.* Upper Fairmount, MD: Art Calendar, 1995.

——, ed. *Getting the Word Out: The Artist's Guide to Self Promotion.* Upper
Fairmount, MD: Art Calendar, 1995.

Gordon, Andrew. "How to Get a Job at Pixar." Creative Bloq, October 25,
2012. www.creativebloq.com/animation/job-at-pixar-10121018.

Jackson, Zella. *The Art of Selling Art,* 2nd ed. Coarsegold, CA: Novasearch
Publishing, 1994.

Ritchie, Bill H., Jr. *The Art of Selling Art: Between Production and Livelihood.*
Seattle, WA: Ritchie's Perfect Press, 1991.

Schumacher, Georgia. "Building a Dynamite Portfolio: How to Present Your Work So It Shines." The Art Institutes. www.artinstitutes.edu/about/blog /building-a-dynamite-portfolio.

Smith, Constance. *Art Marketing 101: A Handbook for the Fine Artist.* Nevada City, CA: ArtNetwork, 2000.

NETWORKING

Artwork Archive. "Is Being Social the Key to Art Business Success?" www.art workarchive.com/blog/is-being-social-the-key-to-art-business-success.

———. "Seven Helpful Networking Tips for Artists." www.artworkarchive .com/blog/7-helpful-networking-tips-for-artists.

Bruce, Kesha. "Networking for Artists Part #1: Changing Your Mind." Fine ArtViews. May 22, 2013. https://fineartviews.com/blog/60349/network ing-for-artists-part-1-changing-your-mind.

———. "Networking for Artists Part #2, Making Connections: How to Start Conversations That Matter." FineArtViews. May 29, 2013. https://fine artviews.com/blog/60641/networking-for-artists-part-2-making-connec tions-how-to-start-conversations-that-matter.

OPEN STUDIO EVENTS

Bhandari, Heather Darcy, and Jonathan Melber. *Art/Work: Everything You Need to Know (and Do) As You Pursue Your Art Career.* New York: Free Press, 2017, 110–18.

Blakeslee, Carolyn, ed. *Getting Exposure: The Artist's Guide to Exhibiting the Work.* Upper Fairmount, MD: Art Calendar, 1995, 80–84.

Horejs, Jason. "Hosting a Successful Open Studio." RedDotBlog. September 22, 2015. https://reddotblog.com/hosting-a-successful-open-studio/.

Michels, Caroll. *How to Survive and Prosper as an Artist: Selling Yourself without Selling Your Soul,* 5th ed. New York: Henry Holt, 2001, 139–40.

Bibliography

Alderson, Rob. "Why Is It Still a Good Idea for Young Creatives to Go to Art School?" It's Nice That. October 6, 2014. www.itsnicethat.com/articles /why-go-to-art-school.

Alic, Nada. "Should You Go to Art School? We Asked 8 Experts to Weigh In." Society6 Blog. May 24, 2016. https://society6.com/studio/blog/should -you-go-to-art-school-we-asked-8-experts-to-weigh-in.

Art Institute of Chicago. "Corpse and Mirror II." www.artic.edu/art works/118981/corpse-and-mirror-ii.

The Art School Guide. "Drawing from Observation." https://artschoolguide .wordpress.com/drawing-from-observation/.

Artopia. "Sculpture—One Minute Art Lesson." Knowitall.org. www.knowitall .org/video/sculpture-one-minute-art-lesson-artopia.

ArtsBridge. "10 College Interview Questions to Ask." https://artsbridge .com/10-college-interview-questions-ask/.

———. "10 College Interview Questions to Expect." https://artsbridge .com/10-college-interview-questions-expect/.

———. "10 Tips for Your Best Art School Portfolio." https://artsbridge.com/10- tips-for-your-best-art-school-portfolio/.

———. "10 Ways to Blow Your College Admissions Interview." https://arts bridge.com/10-ways-to-blow-your-college-interview/.

Artwork Archive. "Is Being Social the Key to Art Business Success?" www.art workarchive. com/blog/is-being-social-the-key-to-art-business-success.

———. "Seven Helpful Networking Tips for Artists." www.artworkarchive. com/blog/7-helpful-networking-tips-for-artists.

———. "What Does It Take to Make It as an Artist?' www.artwork archive.com/blog/what-does-it-take-to-make-it-as-an-artist.

———. "What Is the Artist's Role in Society?" www.artworkarchive.com/blog /what-is-the-artist-s-role-in-society.

———. "What Motivates Art Collectors? (And How to Use It to Your Advantage)." www.artworkarchive.com/blog/what-motivates-art-collectors-and-how-to-use-it-to-your-advantage.

Atkinson, Karen. "Artist Statement Guidelines." Getting Your Sh*t Together. www.gyst-ink.com/artist-statement-guidelines.

Bamberger, Alan. "Making Art on Commission: Tips for Artists." ArtBusiness .com. www.artbusiness.com/privcom.html.

Bayles, David, and Ted Orland. *Art & Fear: Observations on the Perils (and Rewards) of Artmaking.* Santa Barbara, CA: Capra Press, 1993.

Bhandari, Heather Darcy, and Jonathan Melber. *Art/Work: Everything You Need to Know (and Do) As You Pursue Your Art Career.* New York: Free Press, 2017.

Blakeslee, Carolyn, ed. *Getting Exposure: The Artist's Guide to Exhibiting the Work.* Upper Fairmount, MD: Art Calendar, 1995.

———, ed. *Getting the Word Out: The Artist's Guide to Self Promotion.* Upper Fairmount, MD: Art Calendar, 1995.

Bruce, Kesha. "Networking for Artists Part #1: Changing Your Mind." Fine ArtViews. May 22, 2013. https://fineartviews.com/blog/60349/network ing-for-artists-part-1-changing-your-mind.

———. "Networking for Artists Part #2, Making Connections: How to Start Conversations That Matter." FineArtViews. May 29, 2013. https://fine artviews.com/blog/60641/networking-for-artists-part-2-making-connec tions-how-to-start-conversations-that-matter.

Cameron, Julia. *The Artist's Way: A Spiritual Path to Higher Creativity* (New York: Jeremy P. Tarcher, 2002).

Campbell, Anita. "The Trend of the Artist Entrepreneur" Small Business Trends. November 1, 2017. https://smallbiztrends.com/2008/11/the-trend-of-the-artist-entrepreneur.html.

Castellano, Guiuseppe. "No, GO to Art School." www.gcastellano.com/art tips/2015/4/20/no-go-to-art-school.

"Daniel." "The Difficulties of Defining Textile Art." TextileArtist.org. www .textileartist.org/the-difficulties-of-defining-textile-art.

Day, Steve. "How to Get Hired at an Animation Studio." Whiteboard Ani- mation. www.whiteboardanimation.com/blog/how-to-get-hired-at-an-an imation-studio-in-ten-steps.

Dillard, Steven. Response to question "Why do you collect art?" Quora. April 11, 2013. www.quora.com/Why-do-you-collect-art.

Dodge, Krystle. *What Jobs Can I Get with a Bachelor of Fine Arts Degree?* Degree query. www.degreequery.com/jobs-can-get-bachelor-fine-arts-degree/.

Dorrell, Paul. "Excerpts from Paul's Book, *Living the Artist's Life*." Leopold Gallery. July 23, 2018. www.leopoldgallery.com/excerpts-from-pauls-book-living-the-artists-life/.

Eliasson, Olafur. "Why Art Has the Power to Change the World." World Economic Forum. January 18, 2016. www.weforum.org/agenda/2016/01/why-art-has-the-power-to-change-the-world/.

ExploreHealthCareers.org. "Medical Illustrator/Animator." https://explore healthcareers.org/career/arts-and-humanities-in-health/medical-illustrator-animator/.

Gale, Amiria. "How to Make an Art Portfolio for College or University (The Ultimate Guide)." Student Art Guide. October 19, 2018. www.student artguide.com/articles/how-to-make-an-art-portfolio-for-college-or-university.

Garner, Christine. "Traditional Art Mediums." Medium. September 7, 2018. https://medium.com/the-art-squirrel/traditional-art-mediums-4d38f 4da88ce.

Gordon, Andrew. "How to Get a Job at Pixar." Creative Bloq. October 25, 2012. www.creativebloq.com/animation/job-at-pixar-10121018.

Graham, Jenny. "Amber Stanton's Art." Jenny by Design. April 3, 2013. www .jennybydesign.com/amber-stantons-art/.

Grant, Daniel. *Selling Art without Galleries: Toward Making a Living from Your Art.* New York: Allworth Press, 2006.

Gratz, Roberta Brandes. "Daily Close-up, After the Flag." *New York Post*, December 30, 1970.

Hammond, Lee. "Why We Make Art." ArtistsNetwork. www.artistsnetwork .com/art-inspiration/why-we-make-art-lee-hammond/.

Hemmings, Jessica. "Defining a Movement: Textile and Fibre Art." Jessica Hemmings. September 1, 2005. www.jessicahemmings.com/defining-a-movement-textile-fibre-art/.

Hilliard, Mary. "10 Things You Should Know before Attending Art School." Her Campus. March 17, 2018. www.hercampus.com/high-school/10-things-you-should-know-attending-art-school.

Horejs, Jason. "Hosting a Successful Open Studio." RedDotBlog. September 22, 2015. https://reddotblog.com/hosting-a-successful-open-studio/.

Jackson, Zella. *The Art of Selling Art.* 2nd ed. Coarsegold, CA: Novasearch Publishing, 1994.

King, Stephen. *On Writing: A Memoir of the Craft.* New York: Pocket Books, 2000.

Larsson, Naomi. "How to Make a Living from Your Art: Young Artists Share Their Stories." *Guardian.* www.theguardian.com/education/2018/oct/30 /how-to-make-a-living-from-your-art-young-artists-share-their-stories.

"Lauren." "Tips for Preparing Your Art School Portfolio." Peterson's. www .petersons.com/blog/tips-for-preparing-your-art-school-portfolio/.

Lawrence, Hannah. "5 Myths about Being an Artist: Debunked." Acceptd. April 30, 2018. https://getacceptd.com/5-myths-about-being-an-artist-de bunked/.

Lents, Nathan H. "Why Do Humans Make Art?" *Psychology Today.* September 5, 2017. www.psychologytoday.com/us/blog/beastly-behavior/201709 /why-do-humans-make-art.

Lieu, Clara. "Ask the Art Prof: What Should You Include in an Art Portfolio for Art School or College Admission?" Clara Lieu. February 6, 2019. https:// claralieu.wordpress.com/2013/03/19/ask-the-art-professor-what-should- you-include-in-an-art-portfolio-for-art-school-or-college/.

Loudon, Sharon, ed. *Living and Sustaining an Artist's Life: Essays by 40 Working Artists.* Bristol, UK: Intellect Books, 2013.

Macres, Christina. "How to Get into Art School." ArtBistro. May 17, 2010. http://artbistro.monster.com/education/articles/10997-how-to-get-into- art-school.

Manes, Cara. "Take an Object: August 22, 2015–February 28, 2016." Museum of Modern Art. www.moma.org/calendar/exhibitions/1549.

Metropolitan Museum of Art. "What Is Printmaking?" www.metmuseum .org/about-the-met/curatorial-departments/drawings-and-prints/materi als-and-techniques/printmaking.

Michelangelo. www.michelangelo.org/michelangelo-quotes.jsp.

Michels, Caroll. *How to Survive and Prosper as an Artist: Selling Yourself without Selling Your Soul,* 5th ed. New York: Henry Holt, 2001.

Nixon, Andrew. "Meet the Artist: Sandra Porter RWA." The Floating Circle. January 13, 2019. https://floatingcircle-rwa.org/2019/01/13/meet-the- artist-sandra-porter-rwa-ma/.

Princeton Review. "A Day in the Life of a Digital Artist." www.princetonreview .com/careers/201/digital-artist.

Quacquarelli Symonds. "What Can You Do with an Art Degree?" www
.topuniversities.com/student-info/careers-advice/what-can-you-do-art-de
gree.

Ritchie, Bill H., Jr. *The Art of Selling Art: Between Production and Livelihood.*
Seattle, WA: Ritchie's Perfect Press, 1991.

Rosenberg, Gigi. *The Artist's Guide to Grant Writing: How to Find Funds and
Write Foolproof Proposals for the Visual, Literary, and Performing Artist.* New
York: Random House, 2010.

Savchuk, Katia. "Why Art School Can Be a Smart Career Move." *Forbes*, September 7, 2015. www.forbes.com/sites/katiasavchuk/2015/08/19/why-
art-school-can-be-a-smart-career-move/#467417ef372f.

Schumacher, Georgia. "Building a Dynamite Portfolio: How to Present Your
Work So It Shines." The Art Institutes. www.artinstitutes.edu/about/blog
/building-a-dynamite-portfolio.

Severson, Dana. "Starting Salary for a Concept Artist." Chron. https://work
.chron.com/starting-salary-concept-artist-video-games-24949.html.

Smith, Constance. *Art Marketing 101: A Handbook for the Fine Artist.* Nevada
City, CA: ArtNetwork, 2000.

Sorensen, Kathie, and Steve Crabtree. "Exactly What Is Talent, Anyway?
Knowledge and Skills Can Be Learned, But Talent Is Enduring." *Gallup
Business Journal*, October 2, 2000. https://news.gallup.com/businessjour
nal/412/exactly-what-talent-anyway.aspx.

Sotheby's. "The Story Behind Jasper Johns's Iconic and Experimental Crosshatched Works." October 17, 2018. www.sothebys.com/en/articles/the-sto
ry-behind-jasper-johnss-iconic-and-experimental-crosshatched-works.

Stanfield, Alyson B. *I'd Rather Be in the Studio: The Artist's No-Excuse Guide to
Self-Promotion.* Golden, CO: Pentas Press, 2011.

Sundquist, Kate. "How to Create a Portfolio for Art School." College Vine.
August 20, 2018. https://blog.collegevine.com/how-to-create-a-portfolio-
for-art-school/.

Tate. "Art Terms." www.tate.org.uk/art/art-terms.

Thompson, Emily. "5 Things You Must Do When Applying to Art College."
Creative Bloq. July 28, 2018. https://www.creativebloq.com/career/how-
get-art-college-5132555.

Thompson, Erin. "Why People Collect Art." Aeon. August 23, 2016. https://
aeon.co/essays/what-drives-art-collectors-to-buy-and-display-their-finds.

Van Gogh, Vincent. Letter from Drenthe to Theo Van Gogh, October 28, 1883. www.webexhibits.org/vangogh/letter/13/336.htm.

visual-arts-cork.com. "Oldest Art." www.visual-arts-cork.com/prehistoric/oldest-art.htm.

visual-arts-cork.com. "Venus of Berekhat Ram." www.visual-arts-cork.com/prehistoric/venus-of-berekhat-ram.htm.

Waldman, Katy. "Does Having a Day Job Mean Making Better Art?" *New York Times Style Magazine*, March 22, 2018. www.nytimes.com/2018/03/22/t-magazine/art/artist-day-job.html.

Wirestone, Clay. "11 Celebrated Artists Who Didn't Quit Their Day Jobs." Mentalfloss, August 11, 2018. http://mentalfloss.com/article/52293/11-celebrated-artists-who-didnt-quit-their-day-jobs.

Zdunek, Jessica. "Tips on Compiling a Portfolio for Art Scholarships." *U.S. News & World Report*, July 7, 2016. www.usnews.com/education/scholarship-search-insider/articles/2016-07-07/tips-on-compiling-a-portfolio-for-art-scholarships.

About the Author

Marcia Santore is a contemporary painter who has exhibited her artwork in solo, juried, and group exhibitions throughout the United States. Her artwork is held in public and private collections in both the United States and abroad. See her artwork at www.marciasantore.com. She is also a writer and editor, and she enjoys writing about interesting people and the fascinating stuff they do. Read her interviews with artists on her blog artYOP! (www.artyop.com), and learn more about her writing at www.amalgamatedstory.com.

EDITORIAL BOARD